Basics of Life

by

James E. Rummel

authorHOUSE®

AuthorHouse™
1663 Liberty Drive, Suite 200
Bloomington, IN 47403
www.authorhouse.com
Phone: 1-800-839-8640

First published by AuthorHouse 4/19/2010

ISBN: 978-1-4389-1504-3 (sc)

Printed in the United States of America
Bloomington, Indiana

This book is printed on acid-free paper.

Contents

Introduction:

Teenagers just worry about being teenagers and getting through grade school and high school. Then they plan what you might want to do with your life given the opportunities in your country, state, and communities. You only live life once, and you want to absorb as much accurate and useful information and experience as you can from your peers, books, magazines, and television to prepare you for years of healthy life ahead. This starts by being a good teenager. That doesn't mean you can't change if you have rough teenage years, it just means you are better prepared for the real world ahead if you can get through your teenage years without injuring yourself or hurting yourself in the many ways possible going through those tough teenage years. As a teenager, you should want to try to stay active within the school that you go to in order to practice your social skills and learn as much as you can about activities that can help you to involve yourself in life for years to come. That is, get you from the young adult years through the later years in life when things usually change drastically for the person who was once of youth. You can build long lasting relationships also that way. Face it, not everyone decides or desires to go to college or teach school, however, they will want the basic skills and philosophies to get through life in order to be content with them, contribute to society, and basically stay out of trouble.

As a teenager you should start to think about things you like and dislike. Think about things that you find that start to interest you, and decide whether these things are good or bad for you, and whether they will keep you out of trouble. This can actually start as an adolescent when your parents started you in activities that you may or may not decide to continue keeping into your teenage or older years. Face it, you may not really decide your likes or dislikes until later on in life or just the fact that your interests may change as you get older. People might suggest trying different things as you get older and older or it may be something you hear about through the media, however, that is usually how interests change, but you have to start somewhere such as with your teenage years. You may find something that interest you as a teenager that will carry you throughout your life or there are other things that you will just plane grow out of. Anyhow, you will find that your teenage years are a very much important part of your life as a whole.

All the other subjects mentioned in this book are learned in grade school through college (if you go to college) and affect every aspect of your life in some form or fashion as you go through life. There are very good books on the information included in this book written by professors and much more can be learned as you get older and older.

Chapter 1 - Basic Needs:

Everyone has the same three basic needs in life of food, water, shelter, clothing and money or trade system. It is how we go about getting these things that makes a difference and what stage of life you are in. As an infant, adolescent, and usually teenager, you depend on your parents to provide these basic needs until you are ready to go live on your own and provide those basic needs for yourself or by someone else. This is important because we should not just take these things for granite. When we are younger, we don't necessarily think of who provides these basic needs, however, we will complain if we don't have them or if we don't like them. That is just natural for people of that age to do. Once they get old enough to provide some of or all of these basic needs on their own they will generally complain less about having them and do their own thing.

There are or things that people have that are considered as luxuries such as television, automobiles, a house full of furniture, etc. however, these are not considered as the basic needs to survive. It is when people covet or are jealous of these luxuries that lead to theft, murder, and a swarm of other sins that break the Ten Commandments. Once an individual starts earning an income before or after completing a higher level of income, they can provide the basic needs for themselves. You should try to put yourself in a position to be able to afford your lifestyle as you get older and older, however, it is important to always live within your means. That is, what you can afford whether you borrow to obtain the luxuries or not. Stealing from others is not an option and is also against the law. Be content, stealing also brings about mistrust and an unsafe environment in which to live. If you have neighbors, you are to live as a civilized society and live by the law.

The basic needs are usually found just about everywhere that is civilized and can be found in different types of climate, terrains, countries, cultures, etc. As civilized countries, one country may help

1

out another country obtain these basic needs because these needs need to be acquired by all. The lifestyle you choose will determine the type of basic needs you provide for yourself and others around you.

Rich people can afford a bigger home, fresher food, water, and better clothing; however, everyone should be able to obtain the basic needs to survive without stealing to get it. If you work, you should, if you are disabled you can collect disability, if you are homeless, there are shelters to provide the basic needs. It takes all of us to make a society work and everyone has their place in life. This doesn't mean we should give up the dream of improving the quality of our basic needs and luxuries if we can afford it. However, everyone should have the basic needs. Wars and battles have been fought over just the basic needs and luxuries, however are largely fought over religion (see chapter on spirituality).

Some people think that transportation is one of the basic needs, and it probably should be, however, it is not needed in order to sustain life as long as you can walk and are in walking distance of these basic needs. That is why it is not included as one of the basic needs. Walking or crawling would be a minimum form of transportation. In addition, your current situation may dictate how your current basic needs are obtained. Such as, if you were sick you may obtain your basic needs by the hospital, etc. Health care may also be considered as one of the basic needs in most societies, however at a minimum it would be considered as paramedic in nature.

Chapter 2 - Schooling Education:

Many people growing up face the age old question of whether to go to school or not after high school. Most people try and should make an effort to get their high school diploma or GED equivalent degree. It is important for kids from grade school to stay focused toward at least getting their high school education because many places won't hire someone without a high school diploma. Choosing a career because the next obstacle as far as whether to further one's education or not. Many people choose not to go to college and many do. Many graduate from college with a Bachelors degree and don't complete their education due to using drugs, alcohol, or other responsibilities. Choosing a career and getting an education is important, however, completing it is even more important than finding employment.

Some people go the whole way through college to get a PHD and many others are satisfied with a Bachelor's or Master's degree. There should be many job opportunities to choose from before determining what level of education is needed for your occupation.

In order to choose a career as a teenager you should read about different occupations and or check your aptitude for different subjects and if given the chance, work in the area of profession before going to further your education. Face it, college isn't for everyone and it is important to have other occupations that provide enough income for those that choose not to go to college. As a general rule of thumb through, your level of income goes up with the amount of schooling you have, as it should. They don't give diplomas away in college usually. So the moral is, make the right choice for the income comfort level you want and then be satisfied with that. In the United States as the land of opportunity, you don't always need a good education to earn a decent living, however, it sure helps. You have to be content with your life choices and abide by the law. If you live right you have a better chance of living long.

If you are good at math, you should probably choose a career in engineering or the sciences. If you have good social skills you should maybe choose something in that field. If you have interests in a certain field, chances are you have an aptitude for that industry and should choose that career path. It shouldn't always be about money, but it should be about the satisfaction you will get in working in that field. Also, many people change fields or career paths along the road through life, so don't be disappointed if the career you choose early on in life is not the same one you end up with before you quite or retire. Sometimes it requires changing jobs to advance your career into what you really want to do, for employment or enjoyment.

Chapter 3 - Habits:

There are good habits and bad habits and the ones that are bad are usually bad for you.

Let's start with the bad habits. Bad habits would be any that are harmful to your health or the health of others. Also, some habits you can get away with until it somehow cause an accident or health problem, and then it is labeled as a bad habit. An example is using a cell phone in a car by the driver while driving a vehicle.

Good habits don't usually cause any trouble and are usually healthy for you in one way or another. It is up to us to choose which habits we will have as part of our lives; however, we hopefully choose the good ones over the bad ones and avoid the involvement or usage of the bad habits.

You can be friends with someone that has bad habits; however, don't allow them to influence you or your decisions about the habits you choose. Choose good habits over bad ones.

Chapter 4 - Medicine/Drugs:

A lot of people interchange the use of medicine with the term drugs. Medicine by definition is considered legal and drugs could be legal or illegal. Take alcohol for instance, it is considered as a legal drug but you have to be careful not to drink too much or get drunk. You especially don't want to get drunk and drive. The legal limit in most states is 0.08 for alcohol. Marijuana has been made legal in some states, however, it is still a federal crime if caught using it. The debate for marijuana is that it can be used for medicinal purposes for usage as a pain killer. The problem with that is that its usage puts THC in the brain which causes abnormal brain functioning. Dopamine levels are increases with usage of marijuana, however, it is like using too much sugar where the body and brain functioning crashes after the high of its usage. Therefore I would avoid its usage all together. Also, too much caffeine or sugar is not good for you if it has a negative effect on your body such as hyperactivity and/or headaches.

Another problem with marijuana is that it can lead to other illegal drugs such as crack, cocaine, barbiturates, and heroin, all of which are known to be bad substances. Therefore all these illegal drugs should be avoided. There are worst things that people could do than smoke marijuana, however, the tar is 25 times worst than smoking cigarettes, both of which cause cancer and are unhealthy for you.

Over the counter medicines and drugs are FDA approved and should only be used as directed by a licensed physician. Different medicines are prescribed for different disorders or illnesses and you have to be careful on how they are mixed. Different people have different symptoms to different medications and not every medicine works the same for all individuals. That is one reason that new medicines are developed annually the other reason is that a certain medication may stop working as the person gets older due to medicine immunity. This has to be discussed with your physician. Good doctors will always listen and work with their patient. It is also good for the patient to educate themselves on the medications that they are taking. Pharmacist usually provides information for the medication when the prescription is filled. If not you can request the information or look it up in a medication reference book.

Chapter 5 - Nutrition:

Good nutrition is one of the most important aspects of good health. There are six basic food groups that are part of the choices for food consumption. They are as follows in order of importance:

1. Bread, cereal, rice, and pasta

2. Vegetables

3. Fruits

4. Meat, poultry, fish, dry beans, eggs, and nuts

5. Milk, yogurt, and cheese

6. Fats, oils, and sweets

For a balanced diet, you should get 6 to 11 servings from the bread, cereal, rice, and pasta group a day. Examples of one serving is one slice of bread, ½ cup of cooked cereal, rice, or pasta, and three to four small crackers. You should get 2 to 4 servings from the fruit group where one serving is 1 whole fruit such as a medium apple, banana, or orange, ¾ cup fruit juice, and ½ cup berries. You should get 3 to 5 servings from the vegetable group where one serving is ½ cup cooked vegetables; ½ cup chopped raw vegetables or one cup leafy raw vegetables. You should get 2 to 3 servings from the meat, poultry, fish, dry beans, eggs, and nuts group where one serving is 2 to 3 oz. cooked beef, chicken, or turkey, ¼ cup tuna, 1 egg, and ½ cup cooked beans. You should get 2 to 3 servings from the milk, yogurt, and cheese group where one serving is 1 cup of milk or yogurt and 1 ½ oz. of cheese. You are to use fats, oils and sweets sparingly. These are the recommendations by the U. S. Department of Agriculture and Health and Human Services.

For healthy living through nutrition and fitness, eat a balanced diet every day, you will feel better and think clearer. Choose a variety of nutritious foods from each food group. Use fats, oils, sweets, and salt sparingly. Drink at least eight 8-oz. glasses of water each day and more when exercising, however, it is most important to drink beverages only when you are thirsty. Avoid high-calorie soft drinks, caffeinated beverages, and alcohol.

Learn to control your appetite and eat three balanced meals a day with healthy snacks in between meals. Take a walk when you're hungry. The energy used by your digestive system will be transferred to your muscles so you won't feel as hungry. The healthy snacks should consist of an apple, carrots, etc. and drink a glass of water or chew sugar-free gum to curb your hunger. Eat slowly to give your stomach time to tell your brain that you've had enough food. Don't take over-the-counter diet pills or appetite suppressants unless your doctor recommends them. Don't snack just because you are bored, nervous, angry, sad, or stressed.

Exercise regularly and choose an exercise you enjoy such as walking or playing sports. If you need to, exercise with a friend to help you stay motivated. Set realistic goals such as how much weight you are going to lose or how often you are going to exercise. Exercise for at least 20 to 30 minutes, three to four times a week. Stop and rest if you feel dizzy or lightheaded, experience pain in your chest or down your arm, or notice any other abnormal physical symptoms.

The bottom line is eating right and exercise regularly. Some people require additional vitamin supplements in order to get enough nutrition in your body. Always talk to your doctor if you feel you are not healthy because it may require blood tests and other diagnosis to get your nutrition right. There are many good nutritionists that can help in designing a diet that is right for you.

Chapter 6 - Health/Exercise/Sports:

Bottom line is that good health means good nutrition and exercise whether it is walking or playing one of the many sports that you can play. For your health you need good doctors and should have an annual checkup as necessary. There are basically four types of doctors at our disposal. They are chiropractors, dentists, general and specialists, and psychiatry and therapists. Dentists should be seen every six months or as needed for cleaning and checkup. Some chiropractors say that you should have a maintenance back adjustment every month especially if you have a very physical type job or feel better when you have the back adjustments. That means that maybe your posture is not right or you are doing something wrong to knock your back out of adjustment. Dentistry is important in order to maintain healthy teeth and you should brush your teeth at least once or twice a day. The dentist will tell you when it is time to get a filling, cap, dentures or other type of dental treatment.

There are two types of doctors, the general or family doctor and then there is the specialists that are required if surgery or some other specialized type of medical attention is needed. Most people go to their general or family doctor first and then are referred to specialists if required for their health.

Psychiatry is used if there are reasons to believe that certain mental health conditions cannot be control or recovered by the use of therapy. Sometimes it requires both therapy and psychiatry in order to maintain good mental health. There are different types of mental health disorders such as depression, anxiety, irritability, etc. and other stress related mood disorders which can be recovered from by the use of cognitive therapy by oneself or therapist. However, if that doesn't work then it may require seeing a good psychiatrist in order to prescribe medications that can help you deal with these mental health disorders. Sometimes there are things that are physical in nature associated with the brain such as a tumor, etc. that may cause mental health disorders and it is important for a psychiatrist to refer you to a specialist or other medical doctor if necessary and run tests such as an MRI or cat scan to determine if there is something physically wrong with the brain. Most psychiatrists are medical doctors that can run all the necessary tests such as blood tests etc. to determine the health of the patient. The important thing is to get the patient back to health by the means of all the medical resources available to find a cure for recovery. If therapy alone doesn't work then medication or other treatment may be necessary. Medication at best is usually only half of the battle for good health. It requires therapy (self or otherwise), good nutrition and exercise, good doctors, good support groups such as family and friends, and an overall good lifestyle, which means staying away from alcohol and drug abuse.

When considering exercise and sports to stay healthy, there are different types of exercises and sports that use different types of muscles and are either cardiovascular or just muscular in nature such as lifting weights. Sports that are cardiovascular are sports such as tennis, racquet ball, volley ball, track and field, soccer, hockey, basketball, etc. Sports that are both physical and cardiovascular are those such as football, baseball, rugby, etc. Exercise machines are usually cardiovascular in nature and exercise different parts of the body. The exercise machine you use should be selected based upon the muscles that you want to exercise. Lifting weights is probably the only form of exercise that is muscular and sedentary and can cause you to become muscle bound. You should mix some form of cardiovascular with muscular to maintain overall muscle strength and good health. Usually it takes 20 to 30 minutes of good daily exercise in order for it to be beneficial. Riding a bicycle is one of the best forms of overall exercises for cardiovascular. You will notice that most bicyclists are usually slender and in good shape if they ride long enough.

Chapter 7 - Appearance:

Appearance is based upon different factors such as religion, culture, age, race, ethnic groups, gender, and environment or where you live within certain parts a country. Culture is usually a factor based upon your race and religion. For instance, people in Germany may dress differently than people in China or black people may dress different than white people, etc. However, people in Germany may be affected by the religion or local culture. Gender is always a factor because normally women wear makeup and men don't. Ethnic groups can play a factor when considering whether men and women wear makeup. For instance, it is common for Indians to wear makeup in both genders; however, men wear known to wear ceremonial makeup.

Age usually plays a big factor because fades are usually started by teenagers and younger adults. People as they get older tend to be more conservative in their appearance; however, that is not necessarily always the case. There is the mid-life crisis factor where some people go through their metamorphous and think they need to be with the young people again or buy sports cars, etc. Women are usually the ones to wear jewelry in most cultures; however, sometimes men are known to wear jewelry also. Rings are usually universal for male and female genders and this is probably due to marriages that exchange rings. Otherwise there is usually some form of shared symbol or jewelry through marriage which has an outward appearance.

Environment or where you live plays a factor because cowboys and cowgirls dress a certain way, farmers in rural areas a different way, suburban's and urbanites another way. Whether you live in the north, south, east, or west usually plays a factor also, especially with buildings, etc. Eskimo's that live in the north would have different dress and appearance than people in say South America. Buildings are usually designed based on the climate that they are built in and a building in a rural or suburb would probably look different than one in an urban area or city. Also, where you live plays a factor on the building materials that are used. A building in the mountains may be built with different materials than one in the valley and one in Africa would probably be built with different materials than one in the United States of America or China. Even within a given country the appearance of people and buildings might be different depending on where you go within the country. It usually depends on the other factors already mentioned.

So when you choose what your appearance is going to be, consider all the factors of religion, culture, age, race, ethnic groups, gender, and environment or where you live within certain parts a country.

Chapter 8 - Spiritual:

Everyone does believe in something whether they realize it or not. Even an atheist that doesn't believe in God Almighty does believe in something, whether it is science, self, etc. What even motivates them becomes their god such as money. This chapter talks about the one Almighty God and how different denominations or beliefs may alter by such beliefs as the ones written in God inspired books such as the Holy Bible, etc. to form a religion based on those beliefs or teachings. This chapter is Christian based although it covers other religions as well.

It is taught that once the covenant was made for a savior to come for our atonement through the Jews that we were left with basically two groups of people, the Jews and the Greeks or Gentiles. It was the Jews that the covenant of the savior was given to for Mary and Joseph to fulfill before the actual birth of Jesus Christ to be everyone's atonement for our sins. The whole population for the earth did start in Genesis with Adam and Eve in the Garden of Eden (known to be in Babylonia which is modern day Iraq) from the beginning of time for man on this earth.

Genealogy for Different Religions:

Adam and Eve were the first humans to be on this earth according to Genesis in the Holy Bible. Years later were when the Great Flood occurred and Noah and his three sons, wives and families were the only ones to remain on the earth after the flood according to Genesis in the Holy Bible. Sometime later was the tower of Babel in Babylonia which is in modern day Iraq when the twelve tribes were formed and the languages mixed up according to Genesis in the Holy Bible. Abraham was from one tribe to also form the twelve tribes of the Jews (see Genesis 49:1-33), the other eleven tribes were considered as the Gentiles (Greeks) (see Galatians 3:26-29). From Abraham was born Isaac and Ishmael and both were blessed by God. However, from Ishmael we have the Muslims (see about Koran) who were blessed to be large in numbers (see Genesis 17:20-27). From Isaac we have the Jews who were given the covenant for the savior to be born from their descendants (see Genesis 21:1-13) and later Joseph was born from Isaac's descendants. Joseph had two sons Manasseh and Ephraim (Genesis 48:1-21). A descendant of Manasseh was Levi who basically is the root of the Mormon religion (see Malachi 3:1-5 also refer to the book of Mormon). From Ephraim's descendants we have Joseph who married Mary who gave birth to Jesus Christ. That was the start of the Christian faith or religion. Jesus always referred to the Greeks as sons of God (see Galatians 3:26-29) and consists of other religions such as the Buddhists and Hindu's etc. The genealogy of Jesus Christ is given in Luke 3:21-38. All who believe in Christ as their savior can be converted to Christians or are considered as Christians if they hold true to the beliefs in the Holy Bible.

Rules for Reading Scriptures in the Holy Bible:

1. Don't take scriptures out of context.

2. Test the statements written by finding text printed using information from the Holy Spirit, Word (Jesus Christ), and Father (Almighty God).

3. Find at least three scriptures form the Holy Bible to support the statements with no contradictions.

4. Pray that the Holy Spirit will verify or bless what is written to be conclusive (Ephesians Chapter 1).

Salvation — what it takes:

1. Trust God and believe

2. Atonement through Jesus Christ for our sins. When we accept Christ into our lives we are to go and sin no more and abide by the Ten Commandments.

3. Ten Commandments (if you break them you are to make reconciliation or restitution)

4. Baptism, Communion, and other sacraments such as marriage

5. Prayer Life, Praise, and Worship

6. Testimony

7. Salvation Safe with the above.

Spiritual Gifts:

The spiritual gifts consist of prayer, prophesy, tongues, interpretation, worship, truth, humble, patience, love, peace, unity, healing, faith, wisdom, knowledge, miraculous powers, discernment, music, revelation, conqueror, maturity, encouragement, teaching, service, mercy, leadership, giving, and craftsman (see Ephesians, 2 Timothy, and 1 Corinthians).

Angels:

There are two named angels in scriptures and they are Gabriel the Archangel who was the messenger of good news and Michael the Archangel who is the conqueror and deliver. The other angel mentioned is the Angel of the Lord who was God's Messenger or Mouthpiece and is probably Jesus Christ. There are also other angels of God, for instance, the destroyer or Passover angel, angels as messengers, angels as ministers, angel that testifies the word of God, angels that perform ceremonies, and angels for little ones. Angels are given the analogy of stars in the sky; however, we are not to worship angels. There are many stories about angels in scriptures.

Other Spiritual Practices:

There are a few other spiritual practices worth mentioning and they are yoga, meditation and prayer, and acupuncture or using pressure points dealing with stress. You can see doctors and take classes on these other spiritual practices and they can be practiced at home.

Cardinal Sins:

The list of cardinal sins is the so called unforgivable sins and there are three main ones. One is placing enmity between a man and a woman, another is mocking the Holy Spirit, and the third is convicting an innocent person. These are all unforgivable in God's judgment and should never be done. Someone is always to have a fair trial using the MEMORYS principle (see pg. 19 ethics) and mocking the Holy Spirit is like mocking God. The example of what happens to someone that puts enmity between a man and woman is given in Genesis where the serpent was cursed by God in the Garden of Eden when it put enmity between Adam and Eve and caused them to sin. Also, you should never mess with children; they are innocent in God's eyes.

Chapter 9 - Philosophies:

Philosophy is the discipline concerned with questions of how one should live (ethics), what sort of things exist (metaphysics), the nature of knowledge (epistemology), and the principles of reasoning (logic). The word Philosophy is from the Ancient Greek word *philosophia* meaning "love of knowledge" or "love of wisdom". There have been many philosophers throughout the course of time ranging from Ancient philosophy to Contemporary philosophy. The philosophers of East and South Asia are discussed in Eastern philosophy, while the philosophers of North Africa and the Middle East, because of their strong interaction with Europe, and are usually considered part of Western philosophy. Philosophy is what people live by and what nations are built on. From philosophy stems many other branches of science, religion, politics, economics, government, etc.

Branches of Philosophy:

There are many branches of philosophy and it is difficult to give an inclusive list of the main divisions of philosophy because various topics have been studied by philosophers at different times. Ethics, metaphysics, epistemology, and logic are usually included. Other topics include politics, aesthetics, and religion. In addition, there are different philosophies for the different academic studies such as philosophy of science, the philosophy of mathematics, and the philosophy of history.

Ethics:

Ethics is a moral philosophy and is concerned with questions of how people ought to act in a society. Plato's early dialogues constitute a search for definitions of virtue. Met ethics is the study of whether ethical value judgments can be objective at all. Ethics can also be conducted within a religious context. If metaphysics and epistemology asks for "What is out there?" and "How do you know?" or "What is your motives?" then Ethics asks "What should we do about it?" Ethics question are either concerned directly with actions (normative ethics), or concerned with Good and Evil in general (metaphysics). In the court room this is important and is the way all things should be judged, based upon MEMORYS principle. That is; what are the Motives, what are the Ethics, what are the Morals, Order for the first three, what do the Records say, did we Yield to the first four, and then finally what is the Solution or sentence for the value judgments.

Metaphysics:

Metaphysics was first studied systematically by Aristotle. He did not use the term; the term emerged because in later editions of Aristotle's works the book on what is now called metaphysics came after Aristotle's study of physics. He first called the subject philosophy or sometimes just wisdom, and says it is the subject that deals with "first causes and the principles of things". The modern meaning of the term is any inquiry dealing with the ultimate nature of what exists. "What is out there?" is a common way of summarizing the nature of metaphysical questions.

Epistemology:

Epistemology is concerned with the nature and scope of knowledge, and whether knowledge is possible. "How do you know?" is the canonical epistemic question.

Logic:

Logic has two broad divisions: mathematical logic or symbolic logic and philosophy of logic or reasoning.

Western philosophy:

The history of Western philosophy is often divided into three periods: Ancient philosophy, Medieval philosophy, and Modern philosophy. Contemporary philosophy came later after the 1960's.

Ancient Greek philosophy:

Ancient Greek philosophy may be divided into the pre-Socratic period, the Socratic period, and the post-Aristotelian period (or Hellenistic period). The pre-Socratic period was characterized by metaphysical speculation, often preserved in the form of grand sweeping statements, such as "All is fire" or "All changes". The Socratic period is named in honor of Socrates, who along with his pupil Plato, revolutionized philosophy through the use of the Socratic Method, which developed the very general philosophical methods of definition, analysis, and synthesis. While no writings of Socrates survive, his influence as a skeptic is conveyed through Plato's works. Plato's writings are often considered basic texts in philosophy as they defined the fundamental issues of philosophy for future generations. These issues and others were taken up by Aristotle, who studied at Plato's school, the Academy, and who often disagreed with what Plato had written.

Medieval philosophy:

Medieval philosophy is the philosophy of Western Europe and the Middle East during what is now known as the medieval era or the Middle Ages, roughly extending from the fall of the Roman Empire to the Renaissance period. Medieval philosophy is defined partly by the rediscovery and further development of classical Greek philosophy and Hellenistic philosophy, and partly by the need to address theological problems and to integrate sacred doctrine (in Islam, Judaism and Christianity) and secular learning.

Some problems discussed throughout this period are the relation of faith to reason, the existence and unity of God, the object of theology and metaphysics, the problems of knowledge, of universals, and of individuation. Philosophers from the middle Ages include ones that are Muslim, Jewish, and Christian.

Modern philosophies:

Modern philosophy is usually considered to begin with the revival of skepticism from Ancient Greek philosophy and the genesis of modern physical science. Descartes brought about the philosophy of rationalism. Later modern philosophy is usually considered to begin after the philosophy of Immanuel Kant at the beginning of the 19th century. German idealists, such as Fichte, Hegel, and Schelling, expanded on the work of Kant by maintaining that the world is constituted by a rational mind-like process, and as such is entirely knowable. After rejecting idealism, other philosophers, many working from outside the university, initiated lines of thought that would occupy academic philosophy in the early and mid-20th century. These philosophies include pragmatism, phenomenology, existentialism, rationalism, and work in ethics which provided the tools for early analytic philosophy.

Rationalism:

Rationalism is any view emphasizing the role or importance of human reason. Extreme rationalism tries to base all knowledge on reason alone. Rationalism typically starts from premises that cannot coherently be denied, then attempts by logical steps to deduce every possible object of knowledge. See writings from Rene Descartes for more information.

Skepticism:

Skepticism is a philosophical attitude that questions the possibility of obtaining any sort of knowledge. It was first articulated by Pyrrho, who believed that everything could be doubted excerpt appearances. Sextus Empiricus describes skepticism as an ability to place antitheses in any manner whatever, appearances and judgments and thus to come first of all to a suspension of judgment and to mental tranquility. Skepticism so conceived is not merely the use of doubt, but is the use of doubt for a particular end a calmness of the soul, or ataraxia. Skepticism poses itself as a challenge to dogmatism, whose believers think they have found the truth.

Idealism:

Idealism is the epistemological doctrine that nothing can be directly known outside of the minds of thinking beings. Or in an alternative stronger form, it is the metaphysical doctrine that nothing exists apart from minds and the contents of minds. In modern Western philosophy, the epistemological doctrine begins as a core tenet of Descartes who stated that what is in the mind is known more reliably than what is known through the senses. The basic five senses are touch, smell, hearing, taste, and sight.

Pragmatism:

Pragmatism was founded in the spirit of finding a scientific concept of truth, which is not dependent on either personal insight (or revelation) or reference to some metaphysical realm. The truth of a statement should be judged by the effect it has on our actions and truth should be seen as that which the whole of scientific enquiry will ultimately agree on. That should probably be seen as a guiding principle more than a definition of what it means for something to be true, though the details of how this principle should be interpreted have been subject to discussion since Peinte first conceived it. Like Rorty many seem convinced that Pragmatism holds that the truth of beliefs does not consist in their correspondence with reality, but in their usefulness and efficacy.

Phenomenology:

Edmund Husserl's phenomenology was an ambitious attempt to lay the foundations for an account of the structure of conscious experience in general. An important part of Husserl's phenomenological project was to show that all conscious acts are directed at r about objective content a feature that Hussrel called intentionality.

Existentialism:

Existentialism given by Kierkegaard's writings was the idealist philosophical system of Hegel which, he thought, ignored or excluded the inner subjective life of living human beings. Kierkegaard, conversely, held that truth is subjectivity, arguing that what is most important in an actual human being are questions dealing with an individual's inner relationship to existence. In particular, Kierkegaard, a Christian, believed that the truth of religious faith was a subjective question and one to be wrestled with passionately.

Realism:

Realism sometimes means the position opposed to the 18th-century Idealism, namely that some things have real existence outside the mind. Classically, however, realism is the doctrine that abstract entities corresponding to universal terms like 'man' have a real existence. It is opposed to nominalism, the view that abstract or universal terms are words only, or denote mental states such as ideas, beliefs, or intentions. The latter position, famously held by William of Ockham, is conceptualism.

Contemporary philosophy:

In the last hundred years, philosophy has increasingly become an activity practiced within the modern research university, and accordingly it has grown more specialized and more distinct from the natural sciences. Much of philosophy in this period concerns itself with explaining the relation between the theories of the natural sciences and the ideas of the humanities or common sense. The two main philosophies of the contemporary era are structuralism and post-structuralism and the analytic tradition.

Structuralism:

Structuralism was started by linguist Ferdinand de Saussure and is the process of analyzing the underlying systems that make them up which both limits and makes them possible. He conceived of one thing in the system standing out from the others in the system, and ideas as being incapable of existence prior to underlying or linguistic structure which articulates thought. That means ideas are built upon identifying needs that potentially use previous ideas. This led continental thought away from humanism, and toward what was termed the decentering of man. Language is no longer spoken by man to express a true inner self, but language speaks to man no matter what your language is.

The analytic tradition:

There is quite a variance on what the true meaning of the analytic tradition philosophy is, however, some say that there are genuine philosophical problems and that philosophy is continuous with science which may change. In a paper Quine criticizes the distinction between analytic and synthetic statements, arguing that a clear conception of analyticity is unattainable, mainly because it changes. He argued for holism, the idea that language, including scientific language, is a set of interconnected sentences, none of which can be verified on its own, rather the sentences in the language depend on each other for their meaning and truth conditions. As a consequence, language as a whole has only a very fine relation to experience, some sentences which refer directly to experience might be somewhat modified by sense impressions, but as the whole of the language is theory laden, for the whole language to be modified, more than this is required. The language in science consists of equations and theory and materials to make them a reality. The language in linguistics changes as the meaning of words changes. A new language would require the development of linguistics for the new language for it to be spoken or written and must have meaning.

Applied philosophy:

The thoughts a society thinks have profound repercussions on what it does. The applied study of philosophy yields applications such as those in ethics – applied ethics in particular – and political philosophy. The political and economic philosophies of Confucius, Sun Zi, Ibn Khaldun, Ibn Rushd, Ibn Taimiyyah, Niccolò Machiavelli, Gottfried Leibniz, John Locke, Jean-Jacques Rousseau, Karl Marx, John Stuart Mill, Mahatma Gandhi, Martin Luther King Jr. and others – all of these have been used to shape and justify governments and their actions.

In the field of philosophy of education, progressive education as championed by John Dewey has had a profound impact on educational practices in the United States in the 20th century. Descendants of this movement include the current efforts in philosophy for children. Carl von Clausewitz's political philosophy of war has had a profound effect on statecraft, international politics, and military strategy in the 20th century, especially in the years around World War II. Logic has become crucially important in mathematics, linguistics, psychology, computer science, and computer engineering.

Other important applications can be found in epistemology, which aid in understanding the requisites for knowledge, sound evidence, and justified belief (important in law, economics, decision theory, and a number of other disciplines). The philosophy of science discusses the underpinnings of the scientific method and has affected the nature of scientific investigation and argumentation. This has profound impacts. For example, the strictly empirical approach of Skinner's behaviorism affected for decades the approach of the American psychological establishment. Deep ecology and animal rights examine the moral situation of humans as occupants of a world that has non-human occupants to consider also. Aesthetics can help to interpret discussions of music, literature, the plastic arts, and the whole artistic dimension of life. In general, the various philosophies strive to provide practical activities with a deeper understanding of the theoretical or conceptual underpinnings of their fields.

Often philosophy is seen as an investigation into an area not sufficiently well understood to be its own branch of knowledge. What were once philosophical pursuits have evolved into the modern day fields such as psychology, sociology, linguistics, and economics, for example. But as such areas of intellectual endeavor proliferate and expand, so will the broader philosophical questions that they generate.

Eastern philosophy:

Many societies have considered philosophical questions and built philosophical traditions based upon each other's works. Eastern and Middle Eastern philosophical traditions have influenced Western philosophers. Russian (which too many people still counts as Western), Jewish, Islamic, African, and recently Latin American philosophical traditions have contributed to, or been influenced by, Western philosophy: yet each has retained a distinctive identity.

The differences between traditions are often well captured by consideration of their favored historical philosophers, and varying stress on ideas, procedural styles, or written language. The subject matter and dialogues of each can be studied using methods derived from the others, and there are significant commonalities and exchanges between them.

Eastern philosophy refers to the broad traditions that originated or were popular in India, Persia, China, Korea, Japan, and to an extent, the Middle East (which overlaps with Western philosophy due to the spread of the Abraham based religions and the continuing intellectual traffic between these societies and Europe.)

Babylonian philosophy:

The origins of Babylonian philosophy can be traced back to the wisdom of early Mesopotamia, which embodied certain philosophies of life, particularly ethics, in the forms of dialectic, dialogs, epic poetry, folklore, hymns, lyrics, prose, and proverbs. The reasoning and rationality of the Babylonians developed beyond empirical observation.

It is possible that Babylonian philosophy had an influence on early Greek philosophy, and later Hellenistic philosophy. The Babylonian text Dialog of Pessimism contains similarities to the agonistic thought of the sophists, the Heraclitean doctrine of contrasts, and the dialogs of Plato, as well as a precursor to the maieutic Socratic method of Socrates and Plato.

Chinese philosophy:

Philosophy has had a tremendous effect on Chinese civilization, and East Asia as a whole. Many of the great philosophical schools were formulated during the Spring and Autumn Period and Warring States Period, and came to be known as the Hundred Schools of Thought. The four most influential of these were Confucianism, Taoism, Mohism, and Legalism. Later on, during the Tang Dynasty, Buddhism from India also became a prominent philosophical and religious discipline. (It should be noted that Eastern thought, unlike Western philosophy, did not express a clear distinction between philosophy and religion.) Like Western philosophy, Chinese philosophy covers a broad and complex range of thought, possessing a multitude of schools that address every branch and subject area of philosophy.

Indian philosophy:

In the history of the Indian subcontinent, following the establishment of an Aryan–Vedic culture, the development of philosophical and religious thought over a period of two millennia gave rise to what came to be called the six schools of astika, or orthodox, Indian or Hindu philosophy. These schools have come to be synonymous with the greater religion of Hinduism, which was a development of the early Vedic religion.

Hindu philosophy constitutes an integral part of the culture of Southern Asia, and is the first of the Dharmic philosophies which were influential throughout the Far East. The great diversity in thought and practice of Hinduism is nurtured by its liberal universalism.

Persian philosophy:

Persian philosophy can be traced back as far as Old Iranian philosophical traditions and thoughts, with their ancient Indo-Iranian roots. These were considerably influenced by Zarathustra's teachings. Throughout Iranian history and due to remarkable political and social influences such as the Macedonian, the Arab, and the Mongol invasions of Persia, a wide spectrum of schools of thought arose. These espoused a variety of views on philosophical questions, extending from Old Iranian and mainly Zoroastrianism-influenced traditions to schools appearing in the late pre-Islamic era, such as Manichaeism and Mazdakism, as well as various post-Islamic schools. Iranian philosophy after Arab invasion of Persia is characterized by different interactions with the Old Iranian philosophy, the Greek philosophy and with the development of Islamic philosophy. The Illumination school and the Transcendent theosophy are regarded as two of the main philosophical traditions of that era in Persia.

African philosophy:

Philosophical traditions, such as African philosophy, are rarely studied by foreign academia. Since emphasis is mainly placed on Western philosophy as a reference point, the study, preservation and dissemination of valuable, but lesser known, non-Western philosophical works face many obstacles. Key African philosophers include the Fulani Usman Dan Fodio, founder of the Sokoto Caliphate of Northern Nigeria and Umar Tall of Senegal; both were prolific Islamic scholars. Another African philosopher worthy of note in the pre-colonial period was Anton Wilhelm Amo. In the post-colonial period, different images of what could be argued as "African" Philosophy from the level of epistemology have risen. These could include the thoughts and enquiries of such individuals as Cheik Anta Diop, Francis Ohanyido, CL Momoh, and Chinweizu.

The philosophy of the modern and contemporary African world, including the Diasporas, is often known as Africana Philosophy. Key philosophers include Frantz Fanon, Kwesi Wiredu, Paget Henry, Lewis Gordon, Mabogo Percy More and many others.

Chapter 10 - Psychology:

Psychology (from Greek: ψυχή, psychē, "soul", "self" or "mind"; and λόγος, logos, "speech" lit. "to talk about the psyche") is an academic and applied discipline involving the scientific study of mental processes and behavior (Psychology studies Human Behavior, not mental processes, Cognitive Psychology studies mental processes, but psychology in general studies human behavior.). There is some tension between scientific psychology (with its program of empirical research) and applied psychology (dealing with a number of areas).

Psychologists attempt to explain the mind and brain in the context of real life. In contrast neurologists utilize a physiological approach. Psychologists study such phenomena as perception, cognition, emotion, personality, behavior, and interpersonal relationships. Psychology also refers to the application of such knowledge to various spheres of human activity including issues related to daily life—e.g. family, education, and work—and the treatment of mental health problems.

In addition to dissecting the brain's implementation of elementary mental functions, psychology also attempts to understand the role these functions play in social behavior and in social dynamics, while incorporating the underlying physiological and neurological processes into its conceptions of mental functioning. Psychology includes many sub-fields of study and application concerned with such areas as human development, sports, health, industry, media, law, and transpersonal psychology.

Cognitive Psychology:

The nature of thought is another core interest in psychology. Cognitive psychology studies cognition, the mental processes underlying behavior. It uses information processing as a framework for understanding the mind. Perception, learning, problem solving, memory, attention, language and emotion are all well researched areas. Cognitive psychology is associated with a school of thought known as cognitive, whose adherents argue for an information processing model of mental function, informed by positivism and experimental psychology.

Cognitive science is a conjoined enterprise of cognitive psychologists, neurobiologists, workers in artificial intelligence, logicians, linguists, and social scientists, and places a slightly greater emphasis on computational theory and formalization.

Both areas can use computational models to simulate phenomena of interest. Because mental events cannot directly be observed, computational models provide a tool for studying the functional organization of the mind. Such models give cognitive psychologists a way to study the "software" of mental processes independent of the "hardware" it runs on, be it the brain or a computer. Also, cognitive looks at the ways of distorted thinking and what roles they play for that person in society.

Cognitive Distorted Thinking:

All or nothing/Black and White/Polarized Thinking:

You think you're good or bad, smart or dumb, a winner or a loser. You need to see shades of gray or the middle ground. No one is 100% successful in everything. Everyone has asserts and imitations.

Overgeneralization:

Because something seems negative, you assume everything will always go wrong. You got a failing grade and decide you'll never graduate. Someone breaks up with you and you decide you'll never have a satisfying relationship.

Filtering (focusing on negative):

You focus on the rubbish (like coffee grounds) and ignore the positives (the flavorful brew). You get 2-A's, 2-B's, and a D. Instead of praising yourself for A's and B's, you torture yourself over the D.

Jumping to Conclusions/Mind Reading/Fortune Telling:

You immediately assume the worst. You think you can read minds. People are whispering or laughing and you know it's about you. You think you're a fortuneteller. I'll never get promoted. You are quick to judge without getting the facts.

Catastrophizing or Magnifying Negatives or Minimizing Positives:

You decide a small setback is a major catastrophe. You were reprimanded at work and are sure you'll be fired. You magnify your faults or the potential pitfalls of a situation and minimize your assets and achievements. You magnify others attributes and ignore your own.

Emotional Reasoning:

You allow feelings to guide your thoughts. You are depressed and decide life is hopeless. If your moods are governed by a chemical imbalance, they are unpredictable and inaccurate.

Shoulds:

Also known as Musts, Ought To's, and Shouldn'ts. You pressure or chastise yourself and others. Who has authority to dictate someone's behavior? You set yourself up for failure or anger. Don't should or yourself or others.

Labeling:

You call yourself, or others, names like incompetent, ignorant, crazy, or lazy. Labels stick in your mind and cause you to give up on yourself, others, relationships and/or situations.

Personalization:

You take something personally that is marginally relevant to you. You're later to work two times. When a memo is distributed about tardiness, you believe it's meant for you alone (forgetting that numerous co-workers come late).

Blaming Others:

You blame others for your joy or misery. If only he'd ask me out I'd be happy. It's all her fault; I'm in a bad mood. What others say or do affects you only with your permission. Happiness is an inside job contingent on your view of self and/or circumstances. Blaming self you take responsibility for people's actions and/or situations beyond your control.

Fields of applied research:

Applied psychology:

Applied psychology encompasses both psychological research that is designed to help individuals overcome practical problems and the application of this research in applied settings. Much of applied psychology research is utilized in other fields, such as business management, product design, ergonomics, nutrition, law and clinical medicine. Applied psychology includes the areas of clinical psychology, industrial and organizational psychology, human factors, psychology and law, health psychology, school psychology, community psychology and others.

Clinical psychology:

Clinical psychology includes the study and application of psychology for the purpose of understanding, preventing, and relieving psychologically-based distress or dysfunction and to promote subjective well-being and personal development. Central to its practice are psychological assessment and psychotherapy, although clinical psychologists may also engage in research, teaching, consultation, forensic testimony, and program development and administration.

Some clinical psychologists may focus on the clinical management of patients with brain injury—this area is known as clinical neuropsychology. In many countries clinical psychology is a regulated mental health profession.

The work performed by clinical psychologists tends to be done inside various therapy models, all of which involve a formal relationship between professional and client—usually an individual, couple, family, or small group—that employs a set of procedures intended to form a therapeutic alliance, explore the nature of psychological problems, and encourage new ways of thinking, feeling, or behaving. The four major perspectives are Psychodynamic, Cognitive Behavioral, Existential-Humanistic, and Systems or Family therapy. There has been a growing movement to integrate these various therapeutic approaches, especially with an increased understanding of issues regarding culture, gender, spirituality, and sexual-orientation. With the advent of more robust research findings regarding psychotherapy, there is growing evidence that most of the major therapies are about of equal effectiveness, with the key common element being a strong therapeutic alliance. Because of this, more training programs and psychologists are now adopting an eclectic therapeutic orientation.

Clinical psychologists do not usually prescribe medication, although there is a growing movement for psychologists to have limited prescribing privileges. In general, however, when medication is warranted many psychologists will work in cooperation with psychiatrists so that clients get all their therapeutic needs met. Clinical psychologists may also work as part of a team with other professionals, such as social workers and nutritionists.

Counseling psychology:

Counseling psychology is a psychology specialty that facilitates personal and interpersonal functioning across the lifespan with a focus on emotional, social, vocational, educational, health-related, developmental, and organizational concerns. Counselors are primarily clinicians, using psychotherapy and other interventions in order to treat clients. Traditionally, counseling psychology has focused more on normal developmental issues and everyday stress rather than psychopathology, but this distinction has softened over time. Counseling psychologists are employed in a variety of settings, including universities, hospitals, schools, governmental organizations, businesses, private practice, and community mental health centers.

Educational psychology:

Educational psychology is the study of how humans learn in educational settings, the effectiveness of educational interventions, the psychology of teaching, and the social psychology of schools as organizations. The work of child psychologists such as Lev Vygotsky, Jean Piaget and Jerome Bruner has been influential in creating teaching methods and educational practices.

Forensic psychology:

Forensic psychology covers a broad range of practices primarily involving courtroom testimony on given issues. Forensic psychologists are appointed by the court to conduct competency to stand trial evaluations, competency to be executed evaluations, sanity evaluations, and involuntary commitment evaluations, provide sentencing recommendations, and sex offender evaluation and treatment evaluations and provide recommendations to the court through written reports and testimony. Most of the questions the court asks the forensic psychologist are not questions of psychology but rather legal questions. For example, there is no definition of sanity in psychology. Rather, sanity is a legal definition that varies from state to state in the United States and from jurisdiction to jurisdiction. Therefore, a prime qualification of a forensic psychologist is an intimate understanding of the law, especially criminal law.

Psychology and Law:

Legal psychology is a research-oriented field populated with researchers from several different areas within psychology (although social and cognitive psychologists are typical). Legal psychologists explore such topics as jury decision-making, eyewitness memory, scientific evidence, and legal policy. The term "legal psychology" has only recently come into use, and typically refers to any non-clinical law-related research.

Health psychology:

Health psychology is the application of psychological theory and research to health, illness and health care. Whereas clinical psychology focuses on mental health and neurological illness, health psychology is concerned with the psychology of a much wider range of health-related behavior including healthy eating, the doctor-patient relationship, a patient's understanding of health information, and beliefs about illness. Health psychologists may be involved in public health campaigns, examining the impact of illness or health policy on quality of life and in research into the psychological impact of health and social care.

Human factors psychology:

Human factors psychology (sometimes called Engineering Psychology) is the study of how cognitive and psychological processes affect our interaction with tools and objects in the environment. The goal of research in human factors psychology is to better design objects by taking into account the limitations and biases of human mental processes and behavior.

Industrial and organizational psychology:

Industrial and organizational psychology (I/O) is among the newest fields in psychology. Industrial Psychology focuses on improving, evaluating, and predicting job performance while Organizational Psychology focuses on how organizations impact and interact with individuals. In 1910, through the works and experiments of Hugo Munsterberg and Walter Dill Scott, Industrial Psychology became recognized as a legitimate part of the social science. Organizational Psychology was not officially added until the 1970s and since then, the field has flourished. The Society for Industrial Organizational Psychology has approximately 3400 professional members and 1900 student members. These two numbers combine to make up only about four percent of the members in the American Psychological Association but the number has been rising since 1939 when there were only one hundred professional I/O psychologists.

I/O psychologists are employed by academic institutions, consulting firms, internal human resources in industries, and governmental institutions. Various universities across the United States are beginning to strengthen their I/O Psychology programs due to the increase of interest and job demand in the field.

Industrial organizational psychologists look at questions regarding things such as who to hire, how to define and measure successful job performance, how to prepare people to be more successful in their jobs, how to create and change jobs so that they are safer and make people happier, and how to structure the organization to allow people to achieve their potential.

School psychology:

School psychology is dedicated to helping students understand the mind socially and emotionally. School psychologists collaborate with educators and professionals to create safe and supportive learning environment for all students that can strengthen connections between home and school. They are trained to be experts in educational and behavioral assessment, intervention, prevention, and consultation, and many have extensive training in research. Currently, school psychology is the only field in which a professional can be called a "psychologist" without a doctoral degree, with the National Association of School Psychologists (NASP) recognizing the Specialist degree as the entry level. This is a matter of controversy as the APA does not recognize anything below a doctorate as the entry level for a psychologist. Specialist-level school psychologists, who typically receive three years of graduate training, function almost exclusively within school systems, while those at the doctoral-level are found in a number of other settings as well, including universities, hospitals, clinics, and private practice.

Research methods:

Research in psychology is conducted in broad accord with the standards of the scientific method, encompassing both qualitative ethological and quantitative statistical modalities to generate and evaluate explanatory hypotheses with regard to psychological phenomena. Where research ethics and the state of development in a given research domain permits, investigation may be pursued by experimental protocols. Psychology tends to be eclectic, drawing on scientific knowledge from other fields to help explain and understand psychological phenomena. Qualitative psychological research utilizes a broad spectrum of observational methods, including action research, ethnography, exploratory statistics, structured interviews, and participant observation, to enable the gathering of rich information unattainable by classical experimentation. Research in humanistic psychology is more typically pursued by ethnographic, historical, and historiography methods.

The testing of different aspects of psychological function is a significant area of contemporary psychology. Psychometric and statistical methods predominate, including various well-known standardized tests as well as those created ad hoc as the situation or experiment requires.

Academic psychologists may focus purely on research and psychological theory, aiming to further psychological understanding in a particular area, while other psychologists may work in applied psychology to deploy such knowledge for immediate and practical benefit. However, these approaches are not mutually exclusive and most psychologists will be involved in both researching and applying psychology at some point during their career. Clinical psychology, among many of the various disciplines of psychology, aims at developing in practicing psychologists' knowledge of and experience with research and experimental methods which they will continue to build up as well as employ as they treat individuals with psychological issues or use psychology to help others.

When an area of interest requires specific training and specialist knowledge, especially in applied areas, psychological associations normally establish a governing body to manage training requirements. Similarly, requirements may be laid down for university degrees in psychology, so that students acquire an adequate knowledge in a number of areas. Additionally, areas of practical psychology, where psychologists offer treatment to others, may require that psychologists be licensed by government regulatory bodies as well.

Chapter 11 – Science:

Science (from the Latin scientia, meaning "knowledge") is the effort to understand, or to understand better, how the physical world works, with observable evidence as the basis of that understanding. It is done through observation of phenomena, and/or through experimentation that tries to simulate events under controlled conditions.

History of science:

Well into the eighteenth century, science and natural philosophy were not quite synonymous, but only became so later with the direct use of what would become known formally as the scientific method, which was earlier developed during the Middle Ages and early modern period in Europe and the Middle East. Prior to the 18th century, however, the preferred term for the study of nature was natural philosophy, while English speakers most typically referred to the study of the human mind as moral philosophy. By contrast, the word "science" in English was still used in the 17th century to refer to the Aristotelian concept of knowledge which was secure enough to be used as a sure prescription for exactly how to do something. In this differing sense of the two words, the philosopher John Locke in An Essay Concerning Human Understanding wrote that "natural philosophy [the study of nature] is not capable of being made a science".

By the early 1800s, natural philosophy had begun to separate from philosophy, though it often retained a very broad meaning. In many cases, science continued to stand for reliable knowledge about any topic, in the same way it is still used in the broad sense in modern terms such as library science, political science, and computer science. In the more narrow sense of science, as natural philosophy became linked to an expanding set of well-defined laws (beginning with Galileo's laws, Kepler's laws, and Newton's laws for motion), it became more popular to refer to natural philosophy as natural science. Over the course of the nineteenth century, moreover, there was an increased tendency to associate science with study of the natural world (that is, the non-human world). This move sometimes left the study of human thought and society (what would come to be called social science) in a linguistic limbo by the end of the century and into the next.

Through the 19th century, many English speakers were increasingly differentiating science (meaning a combination of what we now term natural and biological sciences) from all other forms of knowledge in a variety of ways. The now-familiar expression "scientific method," which refers to the prescriptive part of how to make discoveries in natural philosophy, was almost unused during the early part of the 19th century, but became widespread after the 1870s, though there was rarely totally agreement about just what it entailed. The word "scientist," meant to refer to a systematically-working natural philosopher, (as opposed to an intuitive or empirically-minded one) was coined in 1833 by William Whewell. Discussion of scientists as a special group of people, who did science, even if their attributes were up for debate, grew in the last half of the 19th century. Whatever people actually meant by these terms at first, they ultimately depicted science, in the narrow sense of the habitual use of the scientific method and the knowledge derived from it, as something deeply distinguished from all other realms of human endeavor.

By the twentieth century, the modern notion of science as a special brand of information about the world, practiced by a distinct group and pursued through a unique method was essentially in place. It was used to give legitimacy to a variety of fields through such titles as "scientific" medicine, engineering, advertising, or motherhood. Over the 1900s, links between science and technology also grew increasingly strong. By the end of the century, it is arguable that technology had even begun to eclipse science as a term of public attention and praise. Scholarly studies of science have begun to refer to "techno science" rather than science of technology separately. Meanwhile, such fields as biotechnology and nanotechnology are capturing the headlines. One author has suggested that, in the coming century, "science" may fall out of use, to be replaced by techno science or even by some more exotic label such as "techknowledgy."

Scientific method:

The scientific method seeks to explain the events of nature in a reproducible way, and to use these reproductions to make useful predictions. It is done through observation of natural phenomena, and/or through experimentation that tries to simulate natural events under controlled conditions. It provides an objective process to find solutions to problems in a number of scientific and technological fields.

Based on observations of a phenomenon, a scientist may generate a model. This is an attempt to describe or depict the phenomenon in terms of a logical physical or mathematical representation. As empirical evidence is gathered, a scientist can suggest a hypothesis to explain the phenomenon. This description can be used to make predictions that are testable by experiment or observation using the scientific method. When a hypothesis proves unsatisfactory, it is either modified or discarded.

While performing experiments, Scientists may have a preference for one outcome over another, and it is important that this tendency does not bias their interpretation. A strict following of the scientific method attempts to minimize the influence of a scientist's bias on the outcome of an experiment. This can be achieved by correct experimental design, and a thorough peer review of the experimental results as well as conclusions of a study. Once the experiment results are announced or published, an important cross-check can be the need to validate the results by an independent party.

Once a hypothesis has survived testing, it may become adopted into the framework of a scientific theory. This is a logically reasoned, self-consistent model or framework for describing the behavior of certain natural phenomena. A theory typically describes the behavior of much broader sets of phenomena than a hypothesis—commonly, a large number of hypotheses can be logically bound together by a single theory. These broader theories may be formulated using principles such as parsimony (e.g., "Occam's Razor"). They are then repeatedly tested by analyzing how the collected evidence (facts) compares to the theory. When a theory survives a sufficiently large number of empirical observations, it then becomes a scientific generalization that can be taken as fully verified. These assume the status of a physical law or law of nature.

Despite the existence of well-tested theories, science cannot claim absolute knowledge of nature or the behavior of the subject or of the field of study due to epistemological problems that are unavoidable and preclude the discovery or establishment of absolute truth. Unlike a mathematical proof, a scientific theory is empirical, and is always open to falsification, if new evidence is presented. Even the most basic and fundamental theories may turn out to be imperfect if new observations are inconsistent with them. Critical to this process is making every relevant aspect of research publicly available, which allows ongoing review and repeating of experiments and observations by multiple researchers operating independently of one another. Only by fulfilling these expectations can it be determined how reliable the experimental results are for potential use by others.

Isaac Newton's Newtonian law of gravitation is a famous example of an established law that was later found not to be universal—it does not hold in experiments involving motion at speeds close to the speed of light or in close proximity of strong gravitational fields. Outside these conditions, Newton's Laws remain an excellent model of motion and gravity. Since general relativity accounts for all the same phenomena that Newton's Laws do and more, general relativity is now regarded as a more comprehensive theory.

Science and engineering has built us automobiles, sent man to the moon, and has even sent lunar modules to mars for exploration. Science is in every aspect of our lives.

Mathematics:

Mathematics is essential to many sciences. One important function of mathematics in science is the role it plays in the expression of scientific models. Observing and collecting measurements, as well as hypothesizing and predicting, often require extensive use of mathematics and mathematical models. Calculus may be the branch of mathematics most often used in science, but virtually every branch of mathematics has applications in science, including "pure" areas such as number theory and topology. Mathematics is fundamental to the understanding of the natural sciences and the social sciences, many of which also rely heavily on statistics.

Statistical methods comprised of mathematical techniques for summarizing and exploring data, allow scientists to assess the level of reliability and the range of variation in experimental results. Statistical thinking also plays a fundamental role in many areas of science.

Computational science applies computing power to simulate real-world situations, enabling a better understanding of scientific problems than formal mathematics alone can achieve. According to the Society for Industrial and Applied Mathematics, computation is now as important as theory and experiment in advancing scientific knowledge.

Whether mathematics itself is properly classified as science, it has been a matter of some debate. Some thinkers see mathematicians as scientists, regarding physical experiments as inessential or mathematical proofs as equivalent to experiments. Others do not see mathematics as a science, since it does not require experimental test of its theories and hypotheses. In practice, mathematical theorems and formulas are obtained by logical derivations which presume axiomatic systems, rather than a combination of empirical observation and method of reasoning that has come to be known as scientific method. In general, mathematics is classified as formal science, while natural and social sciences are classified as empirical sciences.

Philosophy of science:

Velocity-distribution data of a gas of rubidium atoms, confirms the discovery of a new phase of matter by the Bose–Einstein condensate.

The philosophy of science seeks to understand the nature and justification of scientific knowledge. It has proven difficult to provide a definitive account of the scientific method that can decisively serve to distinguish science from non-science. Thus there are legitimate arguments about exactly where the borders are, leading to the problem of demarcation. There is nonetheless a set of core precepts that have broad consensus among published philosophers of science and within the scientific community at large.

Science is reasoned-based analysis of sensation upon our awareness. As such, the scientific method cannot deduce anything about the realm of reality that is beyond what is observable by existing or theoretical means. When a manifestation of our reality previously considered supernatural is understood in the terms of causes and consequences, it acquires a scientific explanation.

Some of the findings of science can be very counter-intuitive. Atomic theory, for example, implies that a granite boulder which appears a heavy, hard, solid, grey object is actually a combination of subatomic particles with none of these properties, moving very rapidly in space where the mass is concentrated in a very small fraction of the total volume. Many of humanity's preconceived notions about the workings of the universe have been challenged by new scientific discoveries. Quantum mechanics, particularly, examines phenomena that seem to defy our most basic postulates about causality and fundamental understanding of the world around us. Science is the branch of knowledge dealing with people and the understanding we have of our environment and how it works.

There are different schools of thought in the philosophy of scientific method. Methodological naturalism maintains that scientific investigation must adhere to empirical study and independent verification as a process for properly developing and evaluating natural explanations for observable phenomena. Methodological naturalism, therefore, rejects supernatural explanations, arguments from authority and biased observational studies. Critical rationalism instead holds that unbiased observation is not possible and a demarcation between natural and supernatural explanations is arbitrary; it instead proposes falsifiability as the landmark of empirical theories and falsification as the universal empirical method. Critical rationalism argues for the ability of science to increase the scope of testable knowledge, but at the same time against its authority, by emphasizing its inherent fallibility. It proposes that science should be content with the rational elimination of errors in its theories, not in seeking for their verification (such as claiming certain or probable proof or disproof; both the proposal and falsification of a theory are only of methodological, conjectural, and tentative character in critical rationalism). Instrumentalism rejects the concept of truth and emphasizes merely the utility of theories as instruments for explaining and predicting phenomena.

Critiques:

Karl Popper denied the existence of evidence and of scientific method. Popper holds that there is only one universal method, the negative method of trial and error. It covers not only all products of the human mind, including science, mathematics, philosophy, art and so on, but also the evolution of life.

Philosophical focus:

Historian Jacques Barzun termed science "a faith as fanatical as any in history" and warned against the use of scientific thought to suppress considerations of meaning as integral to human existence. Many recent thinkers, such as Carolyn Merchant, Theodor Adorno and E. F. Schumacher considered that the 17th century scientific revolution shifted science from a focus on understanding nature, or wisdom, to a focus on manipulating nature, i.e. power, and that science's emphasis on manipulating nature leads it inevitably to manipulate people, as well. Science's focus on quantitative measures has led to critiques that it is unable to recognize important qualitative aspects of the world.

The implications of the ideological denial of ethics for the practice of science itself in terms of fraud, plagiarism, and data falsification, has been criticized by several academics. In "Science and Ethics", the philosopher Bernard Rollin examines the ideology that denies the relevance of ethics to science, and argues in favor of making education in ethics part and parcel of scientific training.

The media and the scientific debate:

The mass media face a number of pressures that can prevent them from accurately depicting competing scientific claims in terms of their credibility within the scientific community as a whole. Determining how much weight to give different sides in a scientific debate requires considerable expertise on the issue at hand. Few journalists have real scientific knowledge, and even beat reporters who know a great deal about certain scientific issues may know little about other ones they are suddenly asked to cover.

Epistemological inadequacies:

Psychologist Carl Jung believed that though science attempted to understand all of nature, the experimental method used would pose artificial, conditional questions that evoke only partial answers. Robert Anton Wilson criticized science for using instruments to ask questions that produce answers only meaningful in terms of the instrument, and that there was no such thing as a completely objective vantage point from which to view the results of science.

Scientific community:

The scientific community consists of the total body of scientists, its relationships and interactions. It is normally divided into "sub-communities" each working on a particular field within science.

Fields:

Fields of science are commonly classified along two major lines: natural sciences, which study natural phenomena (including biological life), and social sciences, which study human behavior and societies. These groupings are empirical sciences, which means the knowledge must be based on observable phenomena and capable of being experimented for its validity by other researchers working under the same conditions. There are also related disciplines that are grouped into interdisciplinary and applied sciences, such as engineering and health science. Within these categories are specialized scientific fields that can include elements of other scientific disciplines but often possess their own terminology and body of expertise.

Mathematics, which is sometimes classified within a third group of science called formal science, has both similarities and differences with the natural and social sciences. It is similar to empirical sciences in that it involves an objective, careful and systematic study of an area of knowledge; it is different because of its method of verifying its knowledge, using a priori rather than empirical methods. Formal science, which also includes statistics and logic, is vital to the empirical sciences. Major advances in formal science have often led to major advances in the physical and biological sciences. The formal sciences are essential in the formation of hypotheses, theories, and laws, both in discovering and describing how things work (natural sciences) and how people think and act (social sciences).

The status of social sciences as an empirical science has been a matter of debate since the 20th century (see Positivism dispute). Discussion and debate abound in this topic with some fields like the social and behavioral sciences accused by critics of being unscientific. In fact, many groups of people from academicians like Nobel Prize physicist Percy W. Bridgman, or Dick Richardson, Ph.D.—Professor of Integrative Biology at the University of Texas at Austin, to politicians like U.S. Senator Kay Bailey Hutchison and other co-sponsors, oppose giving their support or agreeing with the use of the label "science" in some fields of study and knowledge they consider non-scientific, ambiguous, or scientifically irrelevant compared with other fields.

Chapter 12 — Economics:

Economics is the branch of social science that studies the production, distribution, and consumption of goods and services. The term economics comes from the Greek for oikos (house) and nomos (custom or law), hence "rules of the house (hold)."

A definition that captures much of modern economics is that of Lionel Robbins in a 1932 essay: "the science which studies human behavior as a relationship between ends and scarce means which have alternative uses." Scarcity means that available resources are insufficient to satisfy all wants and needs. Absent scarcity and alternative uses of available resources, there is no economic problem. The subject thus defined involves the study of choices as they are affected by incentives and resources.

Areas of economics may be divided or classified into various types, including, microeconomics and macroeconomics, positive economics ("what is") and normative economics ("what ought to be"), mainstream economics and heterodox economics, and fields and broader categories within economics.

One of the uses of economics is to explain how economies, as economic systems, work and what the relations are between economic players (agents) in the larger society. Methods of economic analysis have been increasingly applied to fields that involve people (officials included) making choices in a social context, such as crime, education, the family, health, law, politics, religion, social institutions, and war.

Although discussions about production and distribution have a long history, economics in its modern sense as a separate discipline is conventionally dated from the publication of Adam Smith's The Wealth of Nations in 1776. There Smith describes the subject in these practical and exacting terms:

Political economy, considered as a branch of the science of a statesman or legislator, proposes two distinct objects: first, to supply a plentiful revenue or product for the people, or, more properly, to enable them to provide such a revenue or subsistence for themselves; and secondly, to supply the state or commonwealth with revenue sufficient for the public services. It proposes to enrich both the people and the sovereign.

Smith referred to the subject as 'political economy', but that term was gradually replaced in general usage by 'economics' after 1870.

Basic concepts include production possibilities, opportunity cost, opportunity cost, and economic efficiency. Common problems among different types of economies include, what goods to produce and in what quantities (consumption or investment, private goods or public goods, meat or potatoes, etc.), how to produce them (coal or nuclear power, how much and what kind of machinery, who farms or teaches, etc.), and for whom to produce them, reflecting the distribution of income from output.

Opportunity cost has been described as expressing "the basic relationship between scarcity and choice." Scarcity means that choosing more of one good in the aggregate entails doing with less of the other good. Still, in a market economy, movement along the curve can also be described as the choice of the increased output being worth the cost to the agents.

Consistent with the common economic problems listed above, much applied economics in public policy is concerned with determining how the efficiency of an economy can be improved. Recognizing the reality of scarcity and then figuring out how to organize society for the most efficient use of resources has been described as the "essence of economics," where the subject "makes its unique contribution."

Specialization, division of labor, and gains from trade:

Specialization in production is a pervasive feature of economic organization. Its contribution to economic efficiency and technological progress has long been noted. It includes different types of output among farms, manufacturers, and service providers, economies, etc. Among each of these production systems, there may be a corresponding division of labor with each worker having a distinct occupation or doing a specialized task as part of the production effort, and correspondingly different types of capital equipment and differentiated land uses.

Adam Smith's Wealth of Nations (1776) notably discusses the benefits of the division of labor. How individuals can best apply their own labor or any other resource is a central subject in the first book of the series. Smith claimed that an individual would invest a resource, for example, land or labor, so as to earn the highest possible return on it. Consequently, all uses of the resource must yield an equal rate of return (adjusted for the relative riskiness of each enterprise). Otherwise reallocation would result. This idea, wrote George Stigler, is the central proposition of economic theory. French economist Turgot had made the same point in 1766.

In more general terms, it is theorized that market incentives, including prices of outputs and productive inputs, select the allocation of factors of production by comparative advantage, that is, so that (relatively) low-cost inputs are employed to keep down the opportunity cost of a given type of output. In the process, aggregate output increases as a byproduct or by design. Such specialization of production creates opportunities for gains from trade whereby resource owners benefit from trade in the sale of one type of output for other, more highly-valued goods. A measure of gains from trade is the increased output (formally, the sum of increased consumer surplus and producer profits) from specialization in production and resulting trade.

Money:

Money is a means of final payment for goods in most market economies and the unit of account in which prices are typically stated. It includes currency held by the nonbank public and checkable deposits. It has been described as a social convention, like language, useful to one largely because it is useful to others. As a medium of exchange, money facilitates trade. Its economic function can be contrasted with barter (non-monetary exchange). Given a diverse array of produced goods and specialized producers, barter may entail a hard-to-locate double coincidence of wants as to what is exchanged, say apples and a book. By comparison, money can reduce the transaction cost of exchange because of its ready acceptability. Then it is less costly for the seller to accept money in exchange, rather than what the buyer produces.

At the level of an economy, theory and evidence are consistent with a positive relationship running from the total money supply to the nominal value of total output and to the general price level. For this reason, management of the money supply is a key aspect of monetary policy.

Supply and demand:

The theory of demand and supply is an organizing principle to explain prices and quantities of goods sold and changes thereof in a market economy. In microeconomic theory, it refers to price and output determination in a perfectly competitive market. This has served as a building block for modeling other market structures and for other theoretical approaches.

For a given market of a commodity, demand shows the quantity that all prospective buyers would be prepared to purchase at each unit price of the good. Demand is often represented using a table or a graph relating price and quantity demanded. Demand theory describes individual consumers as "rationally" choosing the most preferred quantity of each good, given income, prices, tastes, etc. A term for this is 'constrained utility maximization' (with income as the "constraint" on demand). Here, 'utility' refers to the (hypothesized) preference relation for individual consumers. Utility and income are then used to model hypothesized properties about the effect of a price change on the quantity demanded. The law of demand states that, in general, price and quantity demanded in a given market are inversely related. In other words, the higher the price of a product, the less of it people would be able and willing to buy of it (other things unchanged). As the price of a commodity rises, overall purchasing power decreases (the income effect) and consumers move toward relatively less expensive goods (the substitution effect). Other factors can also affect demand; for example an increase in income will shift the demand curve outward relative to the origin.

Supply is the relation between the price of a good and the quantity available for sale from suppliers (such as producers) at that price. Supply is often represented using a table or graph relating price and quantity supplied. Producers are hypothesized to be profit-maximizes, meaning that they attempt to produce the amount of goods that will bring them the highest profit. Supply is typically represented as a directly proportional relation between price and quantity supplied (other things unchanged). In other words, the higher the price at which the good can be sold, the more of it producers will supply. The higher price makes it profitable to increase production. At a price below equilibrium, there is a shortage of quantity supplied compared to quantity demanded. This pulls the price up. At a price above equilibrium, there is a surplus of quantity supplied compared to quantity demanded. This pushes the price down. The model of supply and demand predicts that for a given supply and demand curve, price and quantity will stabilize at the price that makes quantity supplied equal to quantity demanded. This is at the intersection of the two curves in the graph described above, market equilibrium.

For a given quantity of a good, the price point on the demand curve indicates the value, or marginal utility to consumers for that unit of output. It measures what the consumer would be prepared to pay for the corresponding unit of the good. The price point on the supply curve measures marginal cost, the increase in total cost to the supplier for the corresponding unit of the good. The price in equilibrium is determined by supply and demand. In a perfectly competitive market, supply and demand equate cost and value at equilibrium.

Demand and supply can also be used to model the distribution of income to the factors of production, including labor and capital, through factor markets. In a labor market for example, the quantity of labor employed and the price of labor (the wage rate) are modeled as set by the demand for labor (from business firms etc. for production) and supply of labor (from workers).

Demand and supply are used to explain the behavior of perfectly competitive markets, but their usefulness as a standard of performance extends to any type of market. Demand and supply can also be generalized to explain variables applying to the whole economy, for example, quantity of total output and the general price level, studied in macroeconomics.

Prices and quantities:

Even a currency has a price, its exchange rate in currency markets. Its determination by supply and demand is an important issue in international trade.

In supply-and-demand analysis, price, the going rate of exchange for a good, coordinates production and consumption quantities. Price and quantity have been described as the most directly observable characteristics of a good produced for the market. Supply, demand, and market equilibrium are theoretical constructs linking price and quantity. But tracing the effects of factors predicted to change supply and demand -- and through them, price and quantity -- is a standard exercise in applied microeconomics and macroeconomics. Economic theory can specify under what circumstances price serves as an efficient communication device to regulate quantity. A real-world application might attempt to measure how much variables that increase supply or demand change price and quantity.

Elementary demand-and-supply theory predicts equilibrium but not the speed of adjustment for changes of equilibrium due to a shift in demand or supply. In many areas, some form of "price stickiness" is postulated to account for quantities, rather than prices, adjusting in the short run to changes on the demand side or the supply side. This includes standard analysis of the business cycle in macroeconomics. Analysis often revolves around causes of such price stickiness and their implications for reaching a hypothesized long-run equilibrium. Examples of such price stickiness in particular markets include wage rates in labor markets and posted prices in markets deviating from perfect competition.

Another area of economics considers whether markets adequately take account of all social costs and benefits. An externality is said to occur where there are significant social costs or benefits from production or consumption that are not reflected in market prices. For example, air pollution may generate a negative externality, and education may generate a positive externality (less crime, etc.). Governments often tax and otherwise restrict the sale of goods that have negative externalities and subsidize or otherwise promote the purchase of goods that have positive externalities in an effort to correct the price distortions caused by these externalities.

Marginalism:

Marginalist economic theory, such as above, describes consumers as attempting to reach a most-preferred position, subject to constraints, including income and wealth. It describes producers as attempting to maximize profits subject to their own constraints (including demand for goods produced, technology, and the price of inputs). Thus, for a consumer, at the point where marginal utility of a good, net of price, reaches zero, further increases in consumption of that good stop. Analogously, a producer compares marginal revenue against marginal cost of a good, with the difference as marginal profit. At the point where the marginal profit reaches zero, further increases in production of the good stop. For movement to equilibrium and for changes in equilibrium, behavior also changes "at the margin" -- usually more-or-less of something, rather than all-or-nothing.

Related conditions and considerations apply more generally to any type of economic system, whether market-based or not, where there is scarcity. The marginalist notion of opportunity cost is a device to measure the size of the trade-off between competing alternatives. Such costs, reflected in prices, are used for predicting responses to public-policy changes or disturbances in a market economy. They are also used for evaluating economic efficiency. Similarly, in a centrally planned economy, shadow-price relations must be satisfied for efficient use of resources. There shadow pricing can be used for modeling production units or sectors in relation to objectives of planners.

Economic reasoning:

Economics as a contemporary discipline relies on rigorous styles of argument. Objectives include formulating theories that are simpler, more fruitful, and more reliable than other theories or no theory. Analysis may begin with a simple model which proposes the hypothesis that one variable is explained by another variable. Often an economic hypothesis is only qualitative, not quantitative. That is, the hypothesis implies the direction of a change in one variable, not the size of the change, for a given change of another variable. To clarify, exposition of theory may proceed with an assumption of ceteris paribus, meaning that other explanatory terms besides the one under consideration are held constant. For example, the quantity theory of money predicts an increase in the nominal value of output from an increase in the money supply, ceteris paribus.

Areas and classifications in economics:

Economics is one social science among several but has fields bordering on other areas, including economic geography, economic history, public choice, cultural economics, and institutional economics.

One division of the subject distinguishes two types of economics. Positive economics ("what is") seeks to explain economic phenomena or behavior. Normative economics ("what ought to be," usually as to public policy) prioritizes choices and actions by some set of criteria; such priorities reflect value judgments, including selection of the criteria.

Analysis of the economy:

Areas of economics may be classified in various ways, but an economy is usually analyzed by use of microeconomics or macroeconomics.

Microeconomics:

Microeconomics examines the economic behavior of sources (including individuals and firms) and their interactions through individual markets, given scarcity and government regulation. A given market might be for a product, say fresh corn, or the services of a factor of production, say bricklaying. The theory considers aggregates of quantity demanded by buyers and quantity supplied by sellers at each possible price per unit. It weaves these together to describe how the market may reach equilibrium as to price and quantity or respond to market changes over time. This is broadly termed demand-and-supply analysis. Market structures, such as perfect competition and monopoly, are examined as to implications for behavior and economic efficiency. Analysis often proceeds' from the simplifying assumption that behavior in other markets remains unchanged, that is, partial-equilibrium analysis. General-equilibrium theory allows for changes in different markets and aggregates across all markets, including their movements and interactions toward equilibrium.

Macroeconomics:

Macroeconomics examines the economy as a whole to explain broad aggregates and their interactions "top down," that is, using a simplified form of general-equilibrium theory. Such aggregates include national income and output, the unemployment rate, and price inflation and sub aggregates like total consumption and investment spending and their components. It also studies effects of monetary policy and fiscal policy. Since at least the 1960s, macroeconomics has been characterized by further integration as to micro-based modeling of sectors, including rationality of players, efficient use of market information, and imperfect competition. This has addressed a long-standing concern about inconsistent developments of the same subject. Macroeconomic analysis also considers factors affecting the long-term level and growth of national income. Such factors include capital accumulation, technological change and labor force growth.

Mathematical and quantitative methods:

Economics as an academic subject often uses geometric methods, in addition to literary methods. Other general mathematical and quantitative methods are also often used for rigorous analysis of the economy or areas within economics. Such methods include mathematical economics, econometrics, and national accounting.

Mathematical economics:

Mathematical economics refers to application of mathematical methods to represent economic theory or analyze problems posed in economics. It uses such methods as calculus and matrix algebra. Expositors cite its advantage in allowing formulation and derivation of key relationships in an economic model with clarity, generality, rigor, and simplicity. For example, Paul Samuelson's book Foundations of Economic Analysis (1947) identifies a common mathematical structure across multiple fields in the subject.

Econometrics:

Econometrics applies mathematical and statistical methods to analyze data related to economic models. For example, a theory may hypothesize that a person with more education will on average earn more income than a person with less education holding everything else equal. Econometric estimates can estimate the magnitude and statistical significance of the relation. Econometrics can be used to draw quantitative generalizations. These include testing or refining a theory, describing the relation of past variables, and forecasting future variables.

National accounting:

National accounting is a method for summarizing aggregate economic activity of a nation. The national accounts are double-entry accounting systems that provide detailed underlying measures of such information. These include the national income and product accounts (NIPA), which provide estimates for the money value of output and income per year or quarter. NIPA allows for tracking the performance of an economy and its components through business cycles or over longer periods. Price data may permit distinguishing nominal from real amounts, that is, correcting money totals for price changes over time. The national accounts also include measurement of the capital stock, wealth of a nation, and international capital flows.

Selected fields:

Agricultural economics:

Agricultural economics is one the oldest and most established fields of economics. It is the study of the economic forces that affect the agricultural sector and the agricultural sector's impact on the rest of the economy. It is an area of economics that, thanks to the necessity of applying microeconomic theories to complex real world situations, has given rise to many important advances of more general applicability; the role of risk and uncertainty, the behavior of households and links between property rights and incentives. More recently policy areas such as international commodity trade and the environment have been stressed.

Development and growth economics:

Growth economics studies factors that explain economic growth – the increase in output per capita of a country over a long period of time. The same factors are used to explain differences in the level of output per capita between countries. Much-studied factors include the rate of investment, population growth, and technological change. These are represented in theoretical and empirical forms (as in the neoclassical growth model) and in growth accounting. The distinct field of development economics examines economic aspects of the development process in relatively low-income countries focusing on structural change, poverty, and economic growth. Approaches in development economics frequently incorporate social and political factors.

Economic systems:

Economic systems are the branch of economics that studies the methods and institutions by which societies determine the ownership, direction, and allocation of economic resources. An economic system of a society is the unit of analysis. Among contemporary systems at different ends of the organizational spectrum are socialist systems and capitalist systems, in which most production occurs in respectively state-run and private enterprises. In between are mixed economies. A common element is the interaction of economic and political influences, broadly described as political economy. Comparative economic systems studies the relative performance and behavior of different economies or systems.

Environmental economics:

Environmental economics is concerned with issues related to degradation, enhancement, or preservation of the environment. In particular, public bids from production or consumption, such as air pollution, can lead to market failure. The subject considers how public policy can be used to correct such failures. Policy options include regulations that reflect cost-benefit analysis or market solutions that change incentives, such as emission fees or redefinition of property rights. Environmental Economics should not be confused with new schools of economic thought sometimes referred to as ecological economics.

Financial economics:

Financial economics, often simply referred to as finance, is concerned with the allocation of financial resources in an uncertain (or risky) environment. Thus, its focus is on the operation of financial markets, the pricing of financial instruments, and the financial structure of companies.

Game theory:

Game theory is a branch of applied mathematics that studies strategic interactions between agents. In strategic games, agents choose strategies that will maximize their payoff, given the strategies the other sources choose. It provides a formal modeling approach to social situations in which decision makers interact with other sources. Game theory generalizes maximization approaches developed to analyze markets such as the supply and demand model. The field dates from the 1944 classic Theory of Games and Economic Behavior by John von Neumann and Oskar Morgenstern. It has found significant applications in many areas outside economics as usually construed, including formulation of nuclear strategies, ethics, political science, and evolutionary theory.

Industrial organization:

Industrial organization studies the strategic behavior of firms, the structure of markets and their interactions. The common market structures studied include perfect competition, monopolistic competition, various forms of oligopoly, and monopoly.

Information economics:

Information economics examines how information (or a lack of it) affects economic decision-making. An important focus is the concept of information asymmetry, where one party has more or better information than the other. The existence of information asymmetry gives rise to problems such as moral hazard, and adverse selection, studied in contract theory. The economics of information has relevance in many fields, including finance, insurance, contract law, and decision-making under risk and uncertainty.

International economics:

International trade studies the determinants of the flow of goods and services across international boundaries. International finance is a macroeconomic field which examines the flow of capital across international borders, and the effects of these movements on exchange rates. Increased trade in goods, services and capital between countries is a major effect of contemporary globalization.

Labor economics:

Labor economics seeks to understand the functioning of the market and dynamics for labor. Labor markets function through the interaction of workers and employers. Labor economics looks at the suppliers of labor services (workers), the demanders of labor services (employers), and attempts to understand the resulting patterns of wages and other labor income and of employment and unemployment, Practical uses include assisting the formulation of full employment of policies.

James E. Rummel

Law and economics:

Law and economics, or economic analysis of law, is an approach to legal theory that applies methods of economics to law. It includes the use of economic concepts to explain the effects of legal rules, to assess which legal rules are economically efficient, and to predict what the legal rules will be. A seminal article by Ronald Coase published in 1961 suggested that well-defined property rights could overcome the problems of externalities.

Chapter 13 – Political Science:

Political science is a branch of social science that deals with the theory and practice of politics and the description and analysis of political systems and political behavior. Political Science is often described as the study of who gets what, where, when and why. Discovering a proper balance between the individual, the society and its Government for civilization and human progress is paramount.

Fields and subfields of political science include political theory and philosophy, civics and comparative politics, theory of direct democracy, apolitical governance, participatory direct democracy, national systems, cross-national political analysis, political development, international relations, foreign policy, international law, politics, public administration, administrative behavior, public law, judicial behavior, and public policy. Political science also studies power in international relations and the theory of Great powers and Superpowers.

Political science is methodologically diverse. Approaches to the discipline include classical political philosophy, interpretivism, structuralism, and behavioralism, realism, pluralism, and institutionalism. Political science, as one of the social sciences, uses methods and techniques that relate to the kinds of inquiries sought: primary sources such as historical documents and official records, secondary sources such as scholarly journal articles, survey research, statistical analysis, case studies, and model building.

Political scientists study the allocation and transfer of power in decision-making, the roles and systems of governance including governments and international organizations, political behavior and public policies. They measure the success of governance and specific policies by examining many factors, including stability, justice, material wealth, and peace. Some political scientists seek to advance positive theses by analyzing politics. Others advance normative theses, by making specific policy recommendations.

Political Scientists provide the frameworks that journalists, special interest groups, politicians, and the electorate analyze issues. Political scientists may serve as advisers to specific politicians, or even run for office as politicians themselves. Political scientists can be found working in governments, in political parties or as civil servants. They may be involved with non-governmental organizations (NGOs) or political movements. In a variety of capacities, people educated and trained in political science can add value and expertise to corporations. Private enterprises such as think tanks, research institutes, polling and public relations firms often employ political scientists. In the United States, political scientists known as "Americanists" look at a variety of data including elections, public opinion and public policy such as Social Security reform, foreign policy, U.S. congressional power, and the U.S. Supreme Court—to name only a few issues.

History:

Political science is a late arrival in terms of social sciences. However, the discipline has a clear set of antecedents such as moral philosophy, political philosophy, political economy, history, and other fields concerned with normative determinations of what ought to be and with deducing the characteristics and functions of the ideal state. In each historic period and in almost every geographic area, we can find someone studying politics and increasing political understanding.

The antecedents of Western politics can also trace their roots back even earlier than Plato and Aristotle, particularly in the works of Homer, Hesiod, Thucydides, Xenophon, and Euripides. Later, Plato analyzed political systems, abstracted their analysis from more literary- and history- oriented studies and applied an approach we would understand as closer to philosophy. Similarly, Aristotle built upon Plato's analysis to include historical empirical evidence in his analysis.

During the rule of Rome, famous historians such as Polybius, Livy and Plutarch documented the rise of the Roman Republic, and the organization and histories of other nations, while statesmen like Julius Caesar, Cicero and others provided us with examples of the politics of the republic and Rome's empire and wars. The study of politics during this age was oriented toward understanding history, understanding methods of governing, and describing the operation of governments.

With the fall of the Roman Empire, there arose a more diffuse arena for political studies. The rise of monotheism and, particularly for the Western tradition, Christianity, brought to light a new space for politics and political action. Works such as Augustine of Hippo's The City of God synthesized current philosophies and political traditions with those of Christianity, redefining the borders between what was religious and what was political. During the Middle Ages, the study of politics was widespread in the churches and courts. Most of the political questions surrounding the relationship between church and state were clarified and contested in this period.

In the Middle East and later other Islamic areas, works such as the Rubaiyat of Omar Khayyam and Epic of Kings by Ferdowsi provided evidence of political analysis, while the Islamic Aristotelians such as Avicenna and later Maimonides and Averroes, continued Aristotle's tradition of analysis and empiricism, writing commentaries on Aristotle's works.

During the Italian Renaissance, Niccolò Machiavelli established the emphasis of modern political science on direct empirical observation of political institutions and actors. Later, the expansion of the scientific paradigm during the Enlightenment further pushed the study of politics beyond normative determinations.

Studies:

Since Political Science is essentially a study of human behavior, observations in controlled environments are usually not available and impossible to reproduce or duplicate. Because of this Political Scientists seek patterns in the reasons and outcomes for political events so that generalizations and theories can be made. Again, study is still difficult since humans make conscious choices unlike other subjects in science, such as organisms, or even inanimate objects as in physics. Despite the complexities, consensus has been reached on various political topics with the help of proper study.

The advent of political science as a university discipline was marked by the creation of university departments and chairs with the title of political science arising in the late 19th century. In fact, the designation "political scientist" is typically reserved for those with a doctorate in the field. Integrating political studies of the past into a unified discipline is ongoing, and the history of political science has provided a rich field for the growth of both normative and positive political science, with each part of the discipline sharing some historical predecessors. The American Political Science Association was founded in 1903 and the American Political Science Review was founded in 1906 in an effort to distinguish the study of politics from economics and other social phenomena.

In the 1950s and the 1960s, a behavioral revolution stressing the systematic and rigorously scientific study of individual and group behavior swept the discipline. At the same time that political science moved toward greater depth of analysis, it also moved toward a closer working relationship with other disciplines, especially sociology, economics, history, anthropology, psychology, public administration and statistics. Increasingly, students of political behavior have used the scientific method to create an intellectual discipline based on the postulating of hypotheses followed by empirical verification and the inference of political trends, and of generalizations that explain individual and group political actions. Over the past generation, the discipline placed an increasing emphasis on relevance, or the use of new approaches and methodologies to solve political and social problems.

Political science has, broadly, five subfields: international relations, political theory, public policy and public administration, national politics, and comparative politics. Separate degree granting programs in international relations and public policy are not uncommon at both the undergraduate and graduate levels. Master's level programs in public administration are common. Political science understands the need and application of different points of view that might make up different parties in a political system.

Chapter 14 – War:

War is any large scale, violent conflict. The conduct of war extends along a continuum, from the almost universal tribal warfare that began well before recorded human history, to wars between city states, nations, or empires. By extension, the word is now used for any struggle, as in the war on drugs or the war on terror. It was once thought humans were the only creatures who fought wars, but closer observation of animal life has discovered wars between ant colonies and chimpanzee tribes.

A group of combatants and their support is called an army on land, a navy at sea, and air force in the air. Wars may be prosecuted simultaneously in one or more different theatres. Within each theater, there may be one or more consecutive military campaigns. A military campaign includes not only fighting but also intelligence, troop movements, supplies, propaganda, and other components. Continuous conflict is traditionally called a battle, although this terminology is not always fed to conflicts involving aircraft, missiles or bombs alone, in the absence of ground troops or naval forces. A civil war is the use of force to resolve internal differences.

In War Before Civilization, Lawrence H. Keeley, a professor at the University of Illinois, says that approximately 90-95% of known societies engaged in at least occasional warfare, and many fought constantly.

Factors Leading to War:

A war may begin following an official declaration of war but undeclared wars are common. Any general theory of war must explain not only war but also peace. It must explain not only the wars fought in almost every generation in almost every country in the world, but also the rare instances of extended relative peace, including the Pax Romana and the peace in Europe since World War II.

Motivations for war may be different for those ordering the war than for those undertaking the war. For a state to prosecute a war it must have the support of its leadership, its military forces, and the population. For example, in the Third Punic War, Rome's leaders may have wished to make war with Carthage for the purpose of eliminating a resurgent rival, while the individual soldiers may have been motivated by a wish to end the practice of child sacrifice. Since many people are involved, a war may acquire a life of its own -- from the confluences of many different motivations.

In Why Nations Go to War, by Darian Domer, the author points out that both sides will claim that morality justifies their fight. He also states that the rationale for beginning a war depends on an overly optimistic assessment of the outcome of hostilities (casualties and costs), and on mis-perceptions of the enemy's intentions

Psychological theories:

Psychologists such as E.F.M. Durban and John Bowlby have argued that human beings are inherently violent. While this violence is repressed in normal society, it needs the occasional outlet provided by war. This combines with other notions such as displacement, where a person transfers their grievances into bias and hatred against other ethnic groups, nations, or ideologies. While these theories may have some explanatory value about why wars occur, they do not explain when or how they occur. Nor do they explain the existence of certain human cultures completely devoid of war. If the innate psychology of the human mind is unchanging, these variations are inconsistent. A solution adapted to this problem by militarists such as Franz Alexander is that peace does not really exist. Periods that is seen as peaceful are actually periods of preparation for a later war or when war is suppressed by a state of great power, such as the Pax Britannica.

If war is innate to human nature, as is presupposed by many psychological theories, then there is little hope of ever escaping it. Psychologists have argued that while human temperament allows wars to occur, this only happens when mentally unbalanced people are in control of a nation. This school of thought argues leaders that seek war such as Napoleon, Hitler, and Stalin were mentally abnormal, but fails to explain the thousands of free and presumably sane people who wage wars at their behest.

A distinct branch of the psychological theories of war are the arguments based on evolutionary psychology. This school tends to see war as an extension of animal behavior, such as territoriality and competition. However, while war has a natural cause, the development of technology has accelerated human destructiveness to a level that is irrational and damaging to the species. Humans have similar instincts to that of a chimpanzee but overwhelmingly more powerful. The earliest advocate of this theory was Konrad Lorenz. These theories have been criticized by scholars such as John G. Kennedy, who argue that the organized, sustained war of humans differs more than just technologically from the territorial fights between animals. Ashley Montagu strongly denies such universalistic instinctual arguments, pointing out that social factors and childhood socialization are important in determining the nature and presence of warfare. Thus while human aggression may be a universal occurrence, warfare is not and would appear to have been a historical invention, associated with certain types of human societies.

The Italian psychoanalyst Franco Fornari, a follower of Melanie Klein, thought that war was the paranoid or projective "elaboration" of mourning. (Fornari 1975). Our nation and country play an unconscious maternal role in our feelings, as expressed in the term "motherland." Fornari thought that war and violence develop out of our "love need": our wish to preserve and defend the sacred object to which we are attached, namely our early mother and our fusion with her. For the adult, nations are the sacred objects that generate warfare. Fornari focused upon sacrifice as the essence of war: the astonishing willingness of human beings to die for their country, to give over their bodies to their nation. Fornari called war the "spectacular establishment of a general human situation whereby death assumes absolute value." We are sure that the ideas for which we die must be true, because "death becomes a demonstrative process."

Sociological theories:

Sociology has long been very concerned with the origins of war, and many thousands of theories have been advanced, many of them contradictory. Sociology has thus divided into a number of schools. One, the Primat der Innenpolitik (Primacy of Domestic Politics) school based on the works of Eckart Kehr and Hans-Ulrich Wehler, sees war as the product of domestic conditions, with only the target of aggression being determined by international realities. Thus World War I was not a product of international disputes, secret treaties, or the balance of power but a product of the economic, social, and political situation within each of the states involved.

This differs from the traditional Primat der Außenpolitik (Primacy of Foreign Politics) approach of Carl von Clausewitz and Leopold von Ranke that argues it is the decisions of statesmen and the geopolitical situation that leads to war.

Demographic theories:

Demographic theories can be grouped into two classes, Malthusian theories and youth bulge theories. Malthusian theories see expanding population and scarce resources as a source of violent conflict.

Pope Urban II in 1095, on the eve of the First Crusade, wrote, "For this land which you now inhabit, shut in on all sides by the sea and the mountain peaks, is too narrow for your large population; it scarcely furnishes food enough for its cultivators. Hence it is that you murder and devour one another, that you wage wars, and that many among you perish in civil strife. Let hatred, therefore, depart from among you; let your quarrels end. Enter upon the road to the Holy Sepulcher; wrest that land from a wicked race, and subject it to yourselves."

This is one of the earliest expressions of what has come to be called the Malthusian theory of war, in which wars are caused by expanding populations and limited resources. Thomas Malthus (1766–1834) wrote that populations always increase until they are limited by war, disease, or famine. This theory is thought by Malthusians to account for the relative decrease in wars during the past fifty years, especially in the developed world, where advances in agriculture have made it possible to support a much larger population than was formerly the case, and where birth control has dramatically slowed the increase in population.

Youth bulge theory differs significantly from Malthusian theories. Its adherents see a combination of large male youth cohorts (as graphically represented as a "youth bulge" in a population pyramid) with a lack of regular, peaceful employment opportunities as a risk pool for violence. While Malthusian theories focus on a disparity between a growing population and available natural resources, youth bulge theory focuses on a disparity between non-inheriting, "excess" young males and available social positions within the existing social system of division of labor.

Contributors to the development of youth bulge theory include French sociologist Gaston Bouthoul, U.S. sociologist Jack A. Goldstone , U.S. political scientist Gary Fuller , and German sociologist Gunnar Heinsohn. Samuel Huntington has modified his Clash of Civilizations theory by using youth bulge theory as its foundation. Youth Bulge theories represent a relatively recent development but seem to have become more influential in guiding U.S. foreign policy and military strategy as both Goldstone and Fuller have acted as consultants to the U.S. Government. CIA Inspector General John L. Helgerson referred to youth bulge theory in his 2002 report "The National Security Implications of Global Demographic Change".

According to Heinsohn, who has proposed youth bulge theory in its most generalized form, a youth bulge occurs when 30 to 40 percent of the males of a nation belong to the "fighting age" cohorts from 15 to 29 years of age. It will follow periods with total fertility rates as high as 4-8 children per woman with a 15-29 year delay. A total fertility rate of 2,1 children born by a woman during her lifetime represents a situation of in which the son will replace the father, the daughter the mother. Thus, a total fertility rate of 2,1 represents replacement level, while anything below represents a sub-replacement fertility rate leading to population decline. Total fertility rates above 2,1 will lead to population growth and to a youth bulge. A total fertility rate of 4-8 children per mother implies 2-4 sons per mother. Consequently, one father has to leave not 1, but 2 to 4 social positions (jobs) to give all his sons a perspective for life, which is usually hard to achieve. Since respectable positions cannot be increased at the same speed as food, textbooks and vaccines, many "angry young men" find themselves in a situation that tends to escalate their adolescent anger into violence.

They are demographically superfluous, might be out of work or stuck in a menial job, and often have no access to a legal sex life before a career can earn them enough to provide for a family.

The combination of these stress factors according to Heinsohn usually heads for one of six different exits. They are Violent Crime, Emigration ("non violent colonization"), Rebellion or putsch, Civil war and/or revolution, Genocide (to take over the positions of the slaughtered), and Conquest (violent colonization, frequently including genocide abroad).

Religions and ideologies are seen as secondary factors that are being used to legitimate violence, but will not lead to violence by themselves if no youth bulge is present. Consequently, youth bulge theorists see both past "Christianity" European colonialism and imperialism and today's "Islamist" civil unrest and terrorism as results of high birth rates producing youth bulges. While during the period of European colonialism, European countries had high birthrates and huge youth bulges that fueled colonialist expansion, today Afghanistan, which has a total fertility rate of 6 children per woman and an estimated unemployment rate of 40%, would represent a typical youth bulge country. The Gaza Strip can be seen as another example of youth-bulge-driven violence, especially if compared to Lebanon which is geographically close, yet remarkably more peaceful. Among prominent historical events that have been linked to the existence of youth bulges is the role played by the historically large youth cohorts in the rebellion and revolution waves of early modern Europe, including French Revolution of 1789, and the importance of economic depression hitting the largest German youth cohorts ever in explaining the rise of Nazism in Germany in the 1930s. The 1994 Rwandan Genocide has also been analyzed as following a massive youth bulge.

While the security implications of rapid population growth have been well known since the completion of the National Security Study Memorandum 200 in 1974, neither the U.S. nor the WHO have effectively implemented the recommended preventive measures to control population growth to avert the terror threat they are now facing. Prominent demographer Stephen D. Mumford attributes this to the influence of the Catholic Church.

Youth bulge theories have been criticized as leading to racial, gender and age discrimination.

Evolutionary psychology theories:

Wars are seen as the result of evolved psychological traits that are turned on by either being attacked or by a population perception of a bleak future. The theory accounts for the IRA going out of business, but leads to a dire view of current wars. Studies of endemic violence and tribal warfare in the Highlands of Papua New Guinea demonstrate that intertribal warfare is highest in those parts of the country where population densities are greatest and pressure on land and other resources is thereby maximized. Similarly, evidence of organized warfare in the Ancient World, in pre-dynastic Mesopotamia and in Ancient Egypt, suggests that organized systematic warfare only appeared after population densities had increased, and there was increased pressure upon limited ecological resources. The book "The Most Dangerous Animal: Human Nature and the Origins of War" by David Livingstone Smith is much more relevant for those seeking a view generated by the Evolutionary Psychology methodology.

The paper "Altruism and War" which can be found here is a work written for an academic audience which takes an Evolutionary Psychology viewpoint on war as well, attempting to describe for the first time the entire psychological process from commitment to group to willingness to kill members of another group on one's groups' behalf.

A critical aspect of all true EP based theories of war is the understanding that most or all of the proximate causes of war are little more than excuses that our minds need to fabricate to justify their actions. These justifications take universal forms at every level of human group conflict. They can include: 1)The assertion that the other group presents a threat which must be defended against, 2)The assertion that the other group has provoked the conflict, 3)The assertion that the other group has committed acts which violate morality (such as stealing from your group, raping women, taking premature babies out of incubators), 4)Descriptions of the other group as being threat animals or pathogens (snakes, bears, jackals, cancers, rats, and so on), 5)Asserting that the other is inherently evil, 6)Asserting that the other group are insane or lead by the insane. The other inherent pattern is that positive group definitional attributes are seen as being the opposite of the enemy or rival group.

Evolutionary Psychology hypothesis on war also importantly show that the decision making process is rarely rational, that in fact human belief and decision making processes are often not rational on the whole.

Of course, one side sometimes is simply defending itself. But more often both sides go through a similar and linked psychological process of justification, as above, and an escalating cycle of verbal and then violent action. Such escalation takes place as an effect of our evolved program to punitively punish the other for their transgression through acts which attempt to dissuade them from further transgression, by going well beyond simple tit-for-tat.

Looking for rational causes, as is common in most hypotheses and even in the above mentioned notions of perceived bleak futures, is not the path to understanding war.

Rationalist theories:

Rationalist theories of war assume that both sides to a potential war are rational, which is to say that each side wants to get the best possible outcome for itself for the least possible loss of life and property to its own side. Given this assumption, if both countries knew in advance how the war would turn out, it would be better for both of them to just accept the post-war outcome without having to actually pay the costs of fighting the war. This is based on the notion, generally agreed to by almost all scholars of war since Carl von Clausewitz that wars are reciprocal, that all wars require both a decision to attack and also a decision to resist attack. Rationalist theory offers three reasons why some countries cannot find a bargain and instead resort to war: issue indivisibility, information asymmetry with incentive to deceive, and the inability to make credible commitments.

Issue indivisibility occurs when the two parties cannot avoid war by bargaining because the thing over which they are fighting cannot be shared between them, only owned entirely by one side or the other. Religious issues, such as control over the Temple Mount in Jerusalem, are more likely to be indivisible than economic issues.

A bigger branch of the theory, advanced by scholars of international relations such as Geoffrey Blainey, is the problem of information asymmetry with incentives to misrepresent. The two countries may not agree on who would win a war between them, or whether victory would be overwhelming or merely eked out, because each side has military secrets about its own capabilities. They will not avoid the bargaining failure by sharing their secrets, since they cannot trust each other not to lie and exaggerate their strength to extract more concessions. For example, Sweden made efforts to deceive Nazi Germany that it would resist an attack fiercely, partly by playing on the myth of Aryan superiority and by making sure that Hermann Göring only saw elite troops in action, often dressed up as regular soldiers, when he came to visit.

Intelligence gathering may sometimes, but not always, mitigate this problem. For example, the Argentinian dictatorship knew that the United Kingdom had the ability to defeat them, but their intelligence failed them on the question of whether the British would use their power to resist the annexation of the Falkland Islands. The American decision to enter the Vietnam War was made with the full knowledge that the communist forces would resist them, but did not believe that the guerrillas had the capability to long oppose American forces.

Thirdly, bargaining may fail due to the states' inability to make credible commitments. In this scenario, the two countries might be able to come to a bargain that would avert war if they could stick to it, but the benefits of the bargain will make one side more powerful and lead it to demand even more in the future, so that the weaker side has an incentive to make a stand now.

Rationalist explanations of war can be critiqued on a number of grounds. The assumptions of cost-benefit calculations become dubious in the most extreme genocidal cases of World War II, where the only bargain offered in some cases was infinitely bad. Rationalist theories typically assume that the state acts as a unitary individual, doing what is best for the state as a whole; this is problematic when, for example, the country's leader is beholden to a very small number of people, as in a personalistic dictatorship. Rationalist theory also assumes that the actors are rational, able to accurately assess their likelihood of success or failure, but the proponents of the psychological theories above would disagree.

Rationalist theories are usually explicated with game theory, for example, the Peace War Game, not a war game as such, rather a simulation of economic decisions underlying war.

Economic theories:

Another school of thought argues that war can be seen as an outgrowth of economic competition in a chaotic and competitive international system. In this view wars begin as a pursuit of new markets, of natural resources, and of wealth. Unquestionably a cause of some wars, from the empire building of Britain to the 1941 Nazi invasion of the Soviet Union in pursuit of oil, this theory has been applied to many other conflicts. It is most often advocated by those to the left of the political spectrum, who argue such wars serve the interests of the wealthy but are fought by the poor. Some to the right of the political spectrum may counter that poverty is relative and one poor in one country can be relatively wealthy in another. Such counter arguments become less valid as the increasing mobility of capital and information level the distributions of wealth worldwide, or when considering that it is relative, not absolute, wealth differences that may fuel wars. There are those on the extreme right of the political spectrum who provide support, fascists in particular, by asserting a natural right of the strong to whatever the weak cannot hold by force. Some centrist, capitalist, world leaders, including Presidents of the United States and US Generals, expressed support for an economic view of war.

"Is there any man, is there any woman, let me say any child here that does not know that the seed of war in the modern world is industrial and commercial rivalry?" - Woodrow Wilson, September 11, 1919, St. Louis. "I spent 33 years and four months in active military service and during that period I spent most of my time as a high class muscle man for Big Business, for Wall Street and the bankers. In short, I was a racketeer, a gangster for capitalism." - simultaneously highest ranking and most decorated United States Marine (including two Medals of Honor) Major General Smedley Butler (and a Republican Party primary candidate for the United States Senate) 1935.

"For the corporation executives, the military metaphysic often coincide with their interest in a stable and planned flow of profit; it enables them to have their risk underwritten by public money; it enables them reasonably to expect that they can exploit for private profit now and later, the risky research developments paid for by public money. It is, in brief, a mask of the subsidized capitalism from which they extract profit and upon which their power is based." C. Wright Mills, Causes of world war 3, 1960. "In the councils of government, we must guard against the acquisition of unwarranted influence, whether sought or unsought, by the military-industrial complex. The potential for disastrous rise of misplaced power exists and will persist." - Dwight Eisenhower, Farewell Address, Jan. 17, 1961.

Marxist theories:

The Marxist theory of war argues that all war grows out of the class war. It sees wars as imperial ventures to enhance the power of the ruling class and divide the proletariat of the world by pitting them against each other for contrived ideals such as nationalism or religion. Wars are a natural outgrowth of the free market and class system, and will not disappear until a world revolution occurs.

Political science theories:

The statistical analysis of war was pioneered by Lewis Fry Richardson following World War I. More recent databases of wars and armed conflict have been assembled by the Correlates of War Project, Peter Brecke and the Uppsala Department of Peace and Conflict Research.

There are several different international relations theory schools. Supporters of realism in international relations argue that the motivation of states is the quest for security, to ensure survival. One position, sometimes argued to contradict the realist view, is that there is much empirical evidence to support the claim that states that are democracies do not go to war with each other, an idea known as the democratic peace theory. Other factors included are difference in moral and religious beliefs, economical and trade disagreements, declaring independence, and others.

Another major theory relating to power in international relations and machtpolitik is the Power Transition theory, which distributes the world into a hierarchy and explains major wars as part of a cycle of hegemony being destabilized by a great power which does not support the hegemony' control.

Types of war and warfare:

Just Cause War:

The Just War Theory was asserted as authoritative Catholic Church teaching by the United States Catholic Bishops in their pastoral letter, "'The Challenge of Peace: God's Promise and Our Response," issued in 1983. More recently, the Catechism of the Catholic Church, 2309, published in 1994, lists four "strict conditions for legitimate defense by military force.

By cause:

Marxism succeeded by the Soviet ideology, distinguished the just and unjust war. Just war was considered to be slave rebellions, or national liberation movements, while an unjust war carried the imperialistic character. Smaller armed conflicts are often called riots, rebellions, coups, etc.

When one country sends armed forces to another, allegedly to restore order or prevent genocide, or other crimes against humanity, or to support a legally recognized government against insurgency, that country sometimes refers to it as a police action. This usage is not always recognized as valid, however, particularly by those who do not accept the connotations of the term.

A Fault Line War is a war that is fought between two or more civilizations. The issue at stake in a fault line war is very symbolic for at least one of the groups involved.

Types of warfare:

Conventional warfare is an attempt to reduce an opponent's military capability. It is a war between nation-states and nuclear or biological weapons are not usually used.

Unconventional warfare is an attempt to achieve military victory through acquiescence, capitulation, or clandestine support for one side of an existing conflict.

Nuclear warfare is a war in which nuclear weapons are used.

Civil war is a war where the forces in conflict belong to the same country or empire or other political entity. Asymmetric warfare, is a conflict between two populations of drastically different levels of military mechanization. This type of war often results in guerrilla tactics. Military action produces a very small percentage of air pollution emissions. Intentional air pollution in combat is one of a collection of techniques collectively called chemical warfare. Poison gas as in chemical weapons was principally used during World War I, and resulted in an estimated 91,198 deaths and 1,205,655 injuries. Various treaties have sought to ban its further use. Non-lethal chemical weapons, such as tear gas and pepper spray, are widely used, sometimes with deadly effect.

By style:

Historian Victor Davis Hanson has claimed there exists a unique "Western Way of War", in an attempt to explain the military successes of Western Europe. It originated in Ancient Greece, where, in an effort to reduce the damage that warfare has on society, the city-states developed the concept of a decisive pitched battle between heavy infantry. This would be preceded by formal declarations of war and followed by peace negotiations. In this system constant low-level skirmishing and guerrilla warfare were phased out in favor of a single, decisive contest, which in the end cost both sides less in casualties and property damage. Although it was later perverted by Alexander the Great, this style of war initially allowed neighbors with limited resources to coexist and prosper.

He argues that Western-style armies are characterized by an emphasis on discipline and teamwork above individual bravado. Examples of Western victories over non-Western armies include the Battle of Marathon, the Battle of Gaugamela, the Siege of Tenochtitlan, and the defense of Rorke's Drift.

Warfare environment:

The environment in which a war is fought has a significant impact on the type of combat which takes place, and can include within its area different types of terrain. This in turn means that soldiers have to be trained to fight in specific types of environments and terrains that generally reflect troops' mobility limitations or enablers. These include Arctic warfare or Winter warfare in general, Desert warfare, Jungle warfare, Maneuver warfare, Naval warfare or Aquatic warfare that includes Littoral, Amphibious and Riverine warfare, Sub-aquatic warfare, Mountain warfare sometimes called Alpine warfare, Urban warfare, Air warfare that includes Airborne warfare and Airmobile warfare, Space warfare, Electronic warfare including Radio, Radar and Network warfare, Border warfare a type of limited defensive warfare, Mine warfare a type of static terrain denial warfare, Psychological warfare, Guerilla warfare, Cyber warfare, Energy warfare, Biological warfare, Trench warfare WWI, and Nuclear warfare.

History of war:

There is little agreement about the origins of war. Some believe war has always been with us; others stress the lack of clear evidence for war in our prehistoric past, and the fact that many peaceful, non-military societies have and still do exist.

Originally, war likely consisted of small-scale raiding. Since the rise of the state some 5000 years ago, military activity has occurred over much of the globe. The advent of gunpowder and the acceleration of technological advances led to modern warfare.

The Human Security Report 2005 documented a significant decline in the number and severity of armed conflicts since the end of the Cold War in the early 1990s. However, the evidence examined in the 2008 edition of the Peace and Conflict study indicates that the overall decline in conflicts has stalled.

Morality of war:

Throughout history war has been the source of serious moral questions. Although many ancient nations and some modern ones have viewed war as noble, over the sweep of history, concerns about the morality of war have gradually increased. Today, war is seen by some as undesirable and morally problematic. At the same time, many view war, or at least the preparation and readiness and willingness to engage in war, as necessary for the defense of their country. Pacifists believe that war is inherently immoral and that no war should ever be fought.

The negative view of war has not always been held as widely as it is today. Heinrich von Treitschke saw war as humanity's highest activity where courage, honor, and ability were more necessary than in any other endeavor. Friedrich Nietzsche also saw war as an opportunity for the Übermensch to display heroism, honor, and other virtues. Another supporter of war, Georg Wilhelm Friedrich Hegel, favored it as part of the necessary process required for history to unfold and allow society to progress. At the outbreak of World War I, the writer Thomas Mann wrote, "Is not peace an element of civil corruption and war purification, liberation, an enormous hope?" This attitude has been embraced by societies from Sparta and Rome in the ancient world to the fascist states of the 1930s.

International law recognizes only two cases for a legitimate war:

Wars of defense: when one nation is attacked by an aggressor, it is considered legitimate for a nation to defend itself against the aggressor.

Wars sanctioned by the UN Security Council: when the United Nations as a whole acts as a body against a certain nation. Examples include various peacekeeping operations around the world.

The subset of international law known as the law of war or international humanitarian law also recognizes regulations for the conduct of war, including the Geneva Conventions governing the legitimacy of certain kinds of weapons, and the treatment of prisoners of war. Cases where these conventions are broken are considered war crimes, and since the Nuremberg Trials at the end of World War II the international community has established a number of tribunals to try such cases.

Factors ending a war:

The political and economic circumstances in the peace that follows war usually depends on the "facts on the ground". Where evenly matched adversaries decide that the conflict has resulted in a stalemate, they may cease hostilities to avoid further loss of life and property. They may decide to restore the antebellum territorial boundaries; redraw boundaries at the line of military control, or negotiate to keep or exchange captured territory. Negotiations between parties involved at the end of a war often result in a treaty, such as the Treaty of Versailles of 1919, which ended the First World War.

A warring party that surrenders may have little negotiating power, with the victorious side either imposing a settlement or dictating most of the terms of any treaty. A common result is that conquered territory is brought under the dominion of the stronger military power. An unconditional surrender is made in the face of overwhelming military force as an attempt to prevent further harm to life and property. For example, the Empire of Japan gave an unconditional surrender to the Allies of World War II after the atomic bombings of Hiroshima and Nagasaki (see Surrender of Japan), the preceding massive strategic bombardment of Japan and declaration of war and the immediate invasion of Manchuria by the Soviet Union. A settlement or surrender may also be obtained through deception or bluffing.

Many other wars, however, have ended in complete destruction of the opposing territory, such as the Battle of Carthage of the Third Punic War between the Phoenician city of Carthage and Ancient Rome in 149 BC. In 146 BC the Romans burned the city, enslaved its citizens, and razed the buildings.

Some wars or war-like actions end when the military objective of the victorious side has been achieved. Others do not, especially in cases where the state structures do not exist, or have collapsed prior to the victory of the conqueror. In such cases, disorganized guerilla warfare may continue for a considerable period. In cases of complete surrender conquered territories may be brought under the permanent dominion of the victorious side. A raid for the purposes of looting may be completed with the successful capture of goods. In other cases an aggressor may decide to end hostilities to avoid continued losses and cease hostilities without obtaining the original objective, such as happened in the Iran-Iraq War.

Some hostilities, such as insurgency or civil war, may persist for long periods of time with only a low level of military activity. In some cases there is no negotiation of any official treaty, but fighting may trail off and eventually stop after the political demands of the belligerent groups have been reconciled, a political settlement has been negotiated, or combatants are gradually killed or decide the conflict is futile.

Chapter 15 – Marriage:

Marriage is a personal union between people. This union may also be called matrimony, while the ceremony that marks its beginning is called a wedding and the status created is sometimes called wedlock.

If recognized by the state, by the religion to which the parties belong and/or by society in general, the act of marriage may change the personal status of the individuals in the eyes of those authorities. The status in the eyes of one authority may not be the same as for another. For example, a marriage may be recognized by the state, but not by a church, and vice versa.

Marriage is an institution in which interpersonal relationships (usually intimate and sexual) are sanctioned with governmental, social, or religious recognition. It is often created by a contract or through civil processes. Civil marriage is the legal concept of marriage as a governmental institution, in accordance with marriage laws of the land.

Marriage may take many forms: for example, a union between one man and one woman as husband and wife is a monogamous heterosexual marriage; polygamy — in which a person takes more than one spouse — is common in many societies; and, in some jurisdictions and denominations, a same-sex marriage unites people of the same sex. (Other jurisdictions may not allow this, but instead provide civil unions or domestic partnerships conferring some or all of the benefits of married status.)

People marry for many reasons, but usually one or more of the following: legal, social and economic stability; the formation of a family unit; procreation and the education and nurturing of children; legitimizing sexual relations; public declaration of love; or to obtain citizenship.

A marriage is often declared by a wedding ceremony, which may be performed either by a religious officiate, by a secular government-sanctioned officiator, or (in weddings that have no church or state affiliation) by a trusted friend of the wedding participants. The act of marriage usually creates obligations between the individuals involved, and in many societies, their extended families.

Finding a partner:

In order to get married, it is necessary to find a suitable partner. A partner may be found by the person wishing to be married through the process of courtship. Alternatively, two marriage candidates may be matched by a third party, typically with the match finalized only if both candidates approve of the union. This is known as an arranged marriage.

The choice between courtship and arranged marriage is made by the person seeking marriage or by his or her parents. In some cases, the parents will be ready to enforce an arranged marriage because of cultural tradition or for some other special reason (e.g., dowry). It is worth noting however, that in many cases the person seeking marriage is comfortable with having his or her marriage arranged and, even disregarding parental preference, would freely choose an arranged marriage. Actual forced marriage is common in only a few communities and often attracts harsh criticism even from people who are generally in favor of arranged marriage.

Arranged marriage:

An arranged marriage between Louis XIV of France and Maria Theresa of Spain

A pragmatic (or 'arranged') marriage is made easier by formal procedures of family or group politics. A responsible authority sets up or encourages the marriage; they may, indeed, engage a professional matchmaker to find a suitable spouse for an unmarried person. The authority figure could be parents, family, a religious official, or a group consensus.

In some cases, the authority figure may choose a match for purposes other than marital harmony. Some of the most popular uses of arranged marriage are for dowry or immigration.

Though now a rarity in Western countries, arranged marriages in countries such as India are still prevalent today. In rural villages, the marriage of a child often has much to do with family property. Parents adopt the practice of child marriage and arrange the wedding, sometimes even before the child is born (though this practice was made illegal by the Child Marriage Restraint Act of the Indian Government). In urban India, people use thriving institutions known as Marriage Bureaus or Matrimonial Sites, where candidates register themselves for small fees. A related form of pragmatic marriage, sometimes called a marriage of convenience, involves immigration laws. According to one publisher of information about "green card" marriages, "Every year over 450,000 United States citizens marry foreign-born individuals and petition for them to obtain a permanent residency (Green Card) in the United States." While this is likely an over-estimate, in 2003 alone 184,741 immigrants were admitted to the U.S. as spouses of U.S. citizens.

Recognition:

The parties to a marriage usually seek social recognition for their relationship, and many societies require official approval of a religious or civil body. If recognized by the State, by the religion to which the parties belong and/or by society in general, the act of marriage may change the personal status of the individuals in the eyes of those authorities.

In the early modern era, John Calvin (1509 – 1564) and his Protestant colleague's reformulated Christian marriage through enactment of The Marriage Ordinance of Geneva, which imposes "The dual requirements of state registration and church consecration to constitute marriage."

In England and Wales, Lord Hardwicke's Marriage Act 1753 required a formal ceremony of marriage, thereby curtailing the practice of Fleet Marriage.

In many jurisdictions, a civil marriage ceremony may take place as part of the religious marriage ceremony, although they are theoretically distinct. In most American states, the marriage may be officiated by a priest, minister, rabbi or other religious authority, and in such a case the religious authority also acts as an agent of the state. In some countries, such as France, Spain, Germany, Turkey, Argentina, Japan and Russia, it is necessary to be married by the state separate from (usually before) any religious ceremony, with the state ceremony being the legally binding one. Some states allow civil marriages in circumstances which are not allowed by many religions, such as same-sex marriages or civil unions.

Marriage relationships may also be created by the operation of the law alone, as in common-law marriage, sometimes called "marriage by habit and repute." This is a judicial recognition that two people who have been living as domestic partners are subject to the rights and obligations of a legal marriage. However, in the UK at least, common-law marriage has been abolished and there are no rights available unless a couple marries or enters into a civil partnership. Conversely, there are examples of people who have a religious ceremony that is not recognized by the civil authorities. Examples include widows who stand to lose a pension if they remarry legally, same-sex couples (where same-sex marriage is not legally recognized), some sects which recognize polygamy, retired couples who would lose pension benefits if legally married, Muslim men who wish to engage in polygamy that is condoned in some situations under Islam, and immigrants who do not wish to alert the immigration authorities that they are married either to a spouse they are leaving behind or because the complexity of immigration laws may make it difficult for spouses to visit on a tourist visa.

In Europe, it has traditionally been the churches' office to make marriages official by registering them. Hence, it was a significant step towards a clear separation of church and state and also an intended and sufficient weakening of the Christian churches' role in Germany, when Chancellor Otto von Bismarck introduced the Zivilehe (civil marriage) in 1875. This law made the declaration of the marriage before an official clerk of the civil administration (both spouses affirming their will to marry) the procedure to make a marriage legally valid and effective, and reduced the clerical marriage to an optional private ceremony.

Rights and obligations:

A Ketubah in Aramaic, a Jewish marriage-contract outlining the duties of each partner.

A marriage, by definition, creates rights and obligations on the married parties, and sometimes on relatives as well. These may include giving a husband/wife or his/her family control over a spouse's sexual services, labor, and/or property, giving a husband/wife responsibility for a spouse's debts, giving a husband/wife visitation rights when his/her spouse is incarcerated or hospitalized, giving a husband/wife control over his/her spouse's affairs when the spouse is incapacitated, establishing the second legal guardian of a parent's child, establishing a joint fund of property for the benefit of children, and establishing a relationship between the families of the spouses. These rights and obligations vary considerably between societies, and between groups within society.

Cohabitation:

Marriage is an institution which can join together people's lives in a variety of emotional and economic ways. In many Western cultures, marriage usually leads to the formation of a new household comprising the married couple, with the married couple living together in the same home, often sharing the same bed, but in some other cultures this is not the tradition.

Also, in southwestern China, walking marriages, in which the husband and wife do not live together, have been a traditional part of the Mosuo culture. Walking marriages have also been increasingly common in modern Beijing. Guo Jianmei, director of the center for women's studies at Beijing University, told a Newsday correspondent, "Walking marriages reflect sweeping changes in Chinese society." A similar arrangement in Saudi Arabia, called misyar marriage, also involves the husband and wife living separately but meeting regularly.

Sex and procreation:

A marriage is commonly held to require a sexual relationship, and non-consummation (that is, failure to engage in sex) may be held grounds for an annulment. However, marriage is not a prerequisite for having children, and having children outside of marriage is not uncommon and increasingly socially accepted. In the United States, the National Center for Health Statistics reported that in 1992, 30.1 percent of births were to unmarried women. In 2006, that number had risen to 38.5 percent. Until recently, children born outside of marriage were termed illegitimate and suffered legal disadvantages and social stigma. In recent years the legal relevance of illegitimacy has declined and social acceptance increased, especially in western countries.

There are some married couples who remain childless either by choice or due to infertility or other factors preventing conception or bearing of children. In some cultures, marriage imposes an obligation on women to bear children. In northern Ghana, for example, payment of bride wealth signifies a woman's requirement to bear children, and women using birth control face substantial threats of physical abuse and reprisals.

Most of the world's major religions look with disfavor on sexual relations prior to marriage. Some teach that sexual relations without marriage is fornication. Fornication is sometimes socially discouraged or even criminal. Sex with a married person other than one's spouse is called adultery, and is universally condemned by all major world religions, and has often been and in some jurisdictions continues to be a crime.

Polygamy:

Polygamous marriage, in which a person is married to more than one spouse at one time, is accepted by many societies, though it is far less common than monogamy. Africa has the highest rate of polygamy in the world. In Senegal, for example, nearly 47 percent of marriages are multiple. Polygyny is the typical form of polygamy, while polyandry is rare. Polygamy is normally not permitted in most western countries (see bigamy), though some recognize bona fides polygamous marriages entered into in countries that routinely perform such marriages, such as in a Muslim country.

Anthropologists distinguish between polygamy and group marriage, in which multiple spouses all become married to one another. Group marriage is rare. In the United States, the historic Oneida Colony provides a prominent 19th-century example of a group marriage, though it was not recognized by any civil or religious authority.

Same-sex marriage:

Since 2001, five countries have recognized same-sex marriages for civil purposes, namely the Netherlands, Belgium, Spain, Canada, and South Africa. To avoid the use of the term "marriage", some other countries now provide for civil unions, which are open to couples of the same sex. Civil unions are recognized and accepted in approximately 30 countries. Some countries, such as Israel, Aruba, and the Netherlands Antilles, recognize same-sex marriages lawfully entered into in other countries.

In the United States, Massachusetts is the only state to recognize same-sex marriage under the name marriage. (In Iowa, a district court that struck down the state's Defense of Marriage Act issued a stay on the ruling the next day, only one same sex couple has been married under Iowa law) The California state supreme court's decision to overturn a gay marriage ban in May 2008 is expected to make California the second state to permit gay marriage when the ruling takes effect in June. Civil unions are a separate form of legal union open to couples of the same sex, and in some jurisdictions also to those of opposite sexes who do not want to marry, often carrying the same entailments as marriage, under a different name. Denmark was the first country in the world (in 1989) to extend the rights and responsibilities of marriage to same-sex couples under the name of registered partnership. Civil unions (and registered partnerships) are currently recognized in 24 out of 193 countries worldwide and in some U.S. states. Many U.S. states have adopted referendums or laws that generally restrict marriage recognition to opposite-sex couples. Federally, the U.S. Senate has considered, and failed to pass, a Federal Marriage Amendment.

In Australia, de facto relationships are legally recognized in many, but not all, ways, with some states having registers of de facto relationships, although the federal government has amended existing legislation to specify that only marriages between a man and a woman will be recognized as 'marriages'. As a result, the Australian Capital Territory's 2006 Bill to give civil unions identical status and processes as registered marriages, was repealed by the federal government before it came into effect.

Some religious denominations ceremonially perform civil unions, and recognize them as essentially equivalent to marriage. These developments have created a political and religious reaction in some countries, including in England, where the Church of England, after long debate, officially banned blessings of gay couples by Church of England clergy, and in the United States, where several states have specifically defined marriage as between a man and a woman, often after popular referendums, including the state of Mississippi which passed a constitutional amendment defining marriage as between a man and a woman and refusing to recognize same-sex marriages from other states with 86% of the vote supporting that proposition.

Marriageable age:

The minimum age at which a person is able to lawfully marry, and if parental or other consents are required, varies from country to country.

As early as 1798, Thomas Malthus proposed delaying the age of marriage to alleviate overpopulation.

Kinship restrictions:

Societies have often placed restrictions on marriage to relatives, though the degree of prohibited relationship varies widely. In most societies, marriage between brothers and sisters has been forbidden, with Ancient Egyptian, Hawaiian, and Inca royalty being prominent exceptions. In many societies, marriage between some first cousins is preferred, while at the other extreme, the medieval Catholic Church prohibited marriage even between distant cousins. The present day Catholic Church still maintains a standard of required distance (in both consanguinity and affinity) for marriage.

Social restrictions:

In 2004, the American Anthropological Association released this statement:

The results of more than a century of anthropological research on households, kinship relationships, and families, across cultures and through time, provide no support whatsoever for the view that either civilization or viable social orders depend upon marriage as an exclusively heterosexual institution. Rather, anthropological research supports the conclusion that a vast array of family types, including families built upon same-sex partnerships, can contribute to stable and humane societies.

Many societies, even some with a cultural tradition of polygamy, recognize monogamy as the only valid form of marriage. For example, People's Republic of China shifted from allowing polygamy to supporting only monogamy in the Marriage Act of 1953 after the Communist revolution. Polygamy is practiced illegally by some groups in the United States and Canada, primarily by Mormon fundamentalist sects that separated from the mainstream Latter Day Saints movement after the practice was renounced in 1890. Many African and Islamic societies still allow polygamy.

Today, the term marriage is generally reserved for a union that is formally recognized by the government (although some people disagree). The phrase legally married can be used to emphasize this point. In the United States, there are two methods of receiving legal recognition of a marriage: common law marriage and obtaining a marriage license. The majority of US states do not recognize common law marriage. Other localities may support various types of domestic partnerships.

Many societies have also adopted other restrictions on whom one can marry, such as prohibitions of marrying persons with the same surname, or persons with the same sacred animal. Anthropologists refer to these sorts of restrictions as exogamy. One example is South Korea's general taboo against a man marrying a woman with the same family name. The most common surname in South Korea is Kim (almost 20%); however, there are several branches (or clans) in the Kim surname. (Korean family names are divided into one or more clans.) Only intra-clan marriages are prohibited, as they are considered one type of exogamy. Thus, many "Kim-Kim" couples can be found.

Societies have also at times required marriage from within a certain group. Anthropologists refer to these restrictions as endogamy. An example of such restrictions would be a requirement to marry someone from the same tribe. Racist laws adopted by some societies in the past—such as Nazi-era Germany, apartheid-era South Africa and most of the United States in the nineteenth and the first half of the 20th century—which prohibited marriage between persons of different races could also be considered examples of endogamy. In the U.S., laws banning interracial marriage, which were state laws, were gradually repealed between 1948 and 1967. The U.S. Supreme Court declared all such laws unconstitutional in the case of Loving v. Virginia in 1967.

Weddings:

Couple married in a Shinto ceremony in Takayama, Gifu prefecture.

A marriage may be celebrated with a wedding ceremony, which can be performed by a religious officiator or through a similar government-sanctioned secular process. Despite the ceremony being led by someone else, most religious traditions maintain that the marriage itself is mediated between the two individuals through vows, with the gathered audience witnessing, affirming, and legitimizing the marriage.

The ceremony in which a marriage is enacted and announced to the community is called a wedding. A wedding in which the participants marry in the "eyes of the law" is called a civil marriage. Religions also facilitate weddings, in the "eyes of God". In many European and some Latin American countries, a religious ceremony must be held separate from the civil ceremony. Certain countries, like Belgium, Bulgaria, the Netherlands and Turkey,[42] demand that the civil marriage take place before any religious marriage. In some countries — notably the United States, Canada, the United Kingdom, the Republic of Ireland, Norway and Spain — both ceremonies can be held together; the officiant at the religious and community ceremony also serves as an agent of the state to enact the civil marriage. That does not mean that the state is "recognizing" religious marriages — the "civil" ceremony just takes place at the same time as the religious ceremony. Often this involves simply signing a register during the religious ceremony. If the civil element of the religious ceremony is omitted, no marriage took place in the eyes of the law.

While some countries, such as Australia, permit marriages to be held in private and at any location, others, including England, require that the civil ceremony be conducted in a place specially sanctioned by law (i.e., a church or registry office), and be open to the public. An exception can be made in the case of marriage by special emergency license, which is normally granted only when one of the parties is terminally ill. Rules about where and when persons can marry vary from place to place. Some regulations require that one of the parties reside in the locality of the registry office.

The way in which a marriage is enacted has changed over time, as has the institution of marriage itself. In Europe during the Middle Ages, marriage was enacted by the couple promising verbally to each other that they would be married to each other; the presence of a priest or other witnesses was not required. This promise was known as the "verbum". If made in the present tense (e.g. "I marry you"), it was unquestionably binding; if made in the future tense ("I will marry you"), it would constitute a betrothal, but if the couple proceeded to have sexual relations, the union was a marriage. As part of the Reformation, the role of recording marriages and setting the rules for marriage passed to the state; by the 1600s many of the Protestant European countries had heavy state involvement in marriage. As part of the Counter-Reformation, the Catholic Church added a requirement of witnesses to the promise, which under normal circumstances had to include the priest.

Marriage and religion:

Many religions have broad teachings regarding marriage. Most Christian churches blessing the couple being married; the wedding ceremony sometimes involves a pledge by the community to support the couple's relationship.

Liturgical Christian communions—notably Anglicanism, Catholicism, and Orthodoxy—consider marriage (sometimes termed holy matrimony) to be an expression of grace, termed a sacrament or mystery. In Western ritual, the sacrament is bestowed upon a husband and wife by the spouses themselves, with a bishop, priest, or deacon normally witnessing the union on behalf of the church. In Eastern ritual churches, the clergyman functions as the minister. Western Christians commonly term marriage a vocation, while Eastern Christians term it an ordination and martyrdom, though the theological emphases indicated by the various names are not excluded by the teachings of either tradition. Marriage is commonly celebrated in the context of a Eucharistic service (a nuptial Mass or Divine Liturgy). The sacrament of marriage is indicative of the relationship between Christ and the Church, yet most Reformed Christians would deny the elevation of marriage to the status of a sacrament. Nevertheless it is considered a covenant between spouses before God.

In Judaism, marriage is viewed as a contractual bond commanded by God in which a man and a woman come together to create a relationship in which God is directly involved. Though procreation is not the sole purpose, a Jewish marriage is also expected to fulfill the commandment to have children. The main focus centers on the relationship between the husband and wife. Kabbalistically, marriage is understood to mean that the husband and wife are merging together into a single soul. This is why a man is considered "incomplete" if he is not married, as his soul is only one part of a larger whole that remains to be unified.

Islam also recommends marriage highly; among other things, it helps in the pursuit of spiritual perfection. Age of marriage is whenever the individuals feel ready, financially and emotionally, for marriage. It should also be noted that in Islam, marriage is not a religious concept as it is in many religions, but a civil contract between a man and a woman.

According to Shia Islam marriage doesn't need any witness or official statement or presence in a definite place and its sufficient that man and woman intend to marry with each other and say specific words to each other which led to a religious contract between them and a couple can live with each other as a family without official contract. Of course there are some criteria which should be observed for example woman should be single.

Bahá'u'lláh, the founder of the Bahá'í Faith, recommended that people marry as an assistance to themselves in their well-being, but did not make it obligatory; he explained that it is both a physical and spiritual bond that endures into the afterlife. Shoghi Effendi, the Guardian of the religion, stated that marriage is a foundation for the structure of human society A Bahá'í marriage requires the consent of the couple, and then of all living parents, as to strengthen the ties between the families and avoid enmity.

Hinduism sees marriage as a sacred duty that entails both religious and social obligations. Old Hindu literature in Sanskrit gives many different types of marriages and their categorization ranging from "Gandharva Vivaha" (instant marriage by mutual consent of participants only, without any need for even a single third person as witness) to normal (present day) marriages, to "Rakshasa Vivaha" (marriage performed by abduction of one participant by the other participant, usually, but not always, with the help of other persons). There are elaborate laws in Manusmriti directing which castes and which varnas can marry which castes, and the penalties for breaking these nuptial laws.[citation needed]

For the most part, religious traditions in the world reserve marriage to heterosexual unions, but there are exceptions including Unitarian Universalist, Metropolitan Community Church and some Anglican dioceses and Quaker, United Church of Canada and Reform Jewish congregations.

Marriage and economics:

Historical traditions:

The economics of marriage have changed over time. Historically, in many cultures the family of the bride had to provide a dowry to pay a man for marrying their daughter. In Early Modern Britain, the social status of the couple was supposed to be equal. After the marriage, the entire property (called "fortune") and expected inheritances of the wife belonged only to her husband (a frequent subject in Early Modern British literature); she was often called "his property", which did then include the protection a single woman did not have. In other cultures, the family of the groom had to pay a bride price to the bride's family for the right to marry the daughter. In some cultures, dowries and bride prices are still demanded today. In both cases, the financial transaction takes place between the groom (or his family) and the bride's family; the bride has no part in the transaction and often no choice in whether to participate in the marriage.

In some cultures, dowries were not unconditional gifts. If the groom had other children, they could not inherit the dowry, which had to go to the bride's children. In the event of her childlessness, the dowry had to return to her family, and sometimes not until the groom's death or remarriage. Often the bride was entitled to inherit at least as much as her dowry from her husband's estate.

Morning gifts, which might also be arranged by the bride's father rather than the bride, are given to the bride herself; the name derives from the Germanic tribal custom of giving them the morning after the wedding night. She might have control of this morning gift during the lifetime of her husband, but is entitled to it when widowed. If the amount of her inheritance is settled by law rather than agreement, it may be called dower. Depending on legal systems and the exact arrangement, she may not be entitled to dispose of it after her death, and may lose the property if she remarries. Morning gifts were preserved for many centuries in morganatic marriage, a union where the wife's inferior social status was held to prohibit her children from inheriting a noble's titles or estates. In this case, the morning gift would support the wife and children. Another legal provision for widowhood was jointure, in which property, often land, would be held in joint tenancy, so that it would automatically go to the widow on her husband's death.

Modern conventions:

In many modern legal systems, two people who marry have the choice between keeping their property separate or combining their property. In the latter case, called community property, when the marriage ends by divorce each owns half; if one partner dies the surviving partner owns half and inheritance rules apply to the other half. In many legal jurisdictions, laws related to property and inheritance provide by default for property to pass upon the death of one party in a marriage to the spouse first and secondarily to the children. Wills and trusts can make alternative provisions for property succession.

In some legal systems, the partners in a marriage are "jointly liable" for the debts of the marriage. This has a basis in a traditional legal notion called the "Doctrine of Necessities" whereby a husband was responsible to provide necessary things for his wife. Where this is the case, one partner may be sued to collect a debt for which they did not expressly contract. Critics of this practice note that debt collection agencies can abuse this by claiming an unreasonably wide range of debts to be expenses of the marriage. The cost of defense and the burden of proof is then placed on the non-contracting party to prove that the expense is not a debt of the family. The respective maintenance obligations, both during and eventually after a marriage, are regulated in most jurisdictions; alimony is one such method.

Some have attempted to analyze the institution of marriage using economic theory; for example, anarchy-capitalist economist David Friedman has written a lengthy and controversial study of marriage as a market transaction (the market for husbands and wives).

Taxation:

Most countries use progressive taxes, in which the tax rate is higher for a taxpayer with a higher income. In some of these countries, spouses are allowed to average their incomes; this is advantageous to a married couple with disparate incomes. In order to compensate for this, many countries provide a higher tax bracket for the averaged income of a married couple. While income averaging might still benefit a married couple with a stay-at-home spouse, such averaging would cause a married couple with roughly equal personal incomes to pay more total tax than they would as two single persons. This is commonly called the marriage penalty.

Moreover, when the rates applied by the tax code are not based on averaging the incomes, but rather on the sum of individuals' incomes, higher rates will definitely apply to each individual in two-earner households in progressive tax systems. This is most often the case with high-income taxpayers and is another situation where some consider there to be a marriage penalty.

Conversely, when progressive tax is levied on the individual with no consideration for the partnership, dual-income couples fare much better than single-income couples with similar household incomes. The effect can be increased when the welfare system treats the same income as a shared income thereby denying welfare access to the non-earning spouse. Such systems apply in Australia and Canada, for example.

Hypergyny and isogamy:

In social science, hypergyny refers to the phenomenon in which women tend to marry men that are of slightly higher social status.

In some cultures, women are expected to marry a spouse who is more economically, socially, or politically powerful. Known as hypergyny, this practice is common in India. Though an expected social norm in America, hypergyny is slowly being replaced by isogamy, marriage between equals, and the marrying 'down' of woman.[citation needed] Many anthropologists ascribe this to increased gender equality between women and men.

Termination:

In most societies, the death of one of the partners terminates the marriage, and in monogamous societies this allows the other partner to remarry, though sometimes after a waiting or mourning period. In English speaking countries, the spouse who outlives the other is referred to as a widow (female) or widower (male). Many societies also provide for the termination of marriage through divorce. Marriages can also be annulled in some societies, where an authority declares that a marriage never happened. In Christianity, divorce could lead to adultery if the person who divorces the other partner remarries or has sexual relationship with another partner. There are three Biblical reasons for a divorce. They are Physical abuse, Fornication or adultery, and unevenly yoked meaning unbeliever with believer in God. Irreconcilable differences is not a Biblical reason for a divorce, unless, it is covered by unevenly yoked as just mentioned, that is, believer and unbeliever.

Several cultures have practiced temporary and conditional marriages. Examples include the Celtic practice of hand fasting and fixed-term marriages in the Muslim community. Pre-Islamic Arabs practiced a form of temporary marriage that carries on today in the practice of Nikah Mut'ah, a fixed-term marriage contract. Muslim controversies related to Nikah Mut'ah have resulted in the practice being confined mostly to Shi'ite communities.

Contemporary views on marriage:

Criticisms:

Criticisms of marriage appear as ancient as the institution itself. For example, Plato's Republic's recommendation of group marriage is a famous early critique. Commentators have often been critical of individual local practices and traditions, often leading to changes. Examples include the early Catholic Church's efforts to eliminate concubinage and temporary marriage, the Protestant authorization of divorce, the abolition in the 18th, 19th and 20th century of laws against inter-faith and inter-race marriages in western countries, etc.

Many contemporary critiques have developed from a feminist viewpoint and suggest that modern marriage can be particularly disadvantageous to women economically and socially. Conversely, father's rights advocates claim that there is a continuing societal bias towards women as custodial parents in the face of "no-fault" divorce laws is unjust to men when marriages fail. Some groups, such as the Independent Women's Forum, acknowledge these critiques as valid, but emphasize that they should not be leveled against marriage itself, but dealt with independently.

Controversial views:

Some views about marriage are controversial. Advocates of same-sex rights movements criticize the widespread exclusion of homosexual relationships from the legal and social sanction it provides. At the same time advocates of the so-called traditional marriage movement oppose any attempt to define marriage to include anything other than the union of one man and one woman, claiming that to do so would, "deprive the term of its fundamental and defining meaning."

Chapter 16 – Parenting:

Parenting is the process of raising and educating a child from birth, or before, until adulthood. In the case of humans, it is usually done by the biological parents of the child in question, although governments and society take a role as well. In many cases, orphaned or abandoned children receive parental care from non-parent blood relations. Others may be adopted, raised by foster care, or be placed in an orphanage.

The goals of human parenting are debated. Usually, parental figures provide for a child's physical needs, protect them from harm, and impart in them skills and cultural values until they reach legal adulthood, usually after adolescence. Among non-human species, parenting is usually less lengthy and complicated, though mammals tend to nurture their young extensively. The degree of attention parents invest in their offspring is largely inversely proportional to the number of offspring the average adult in the species produces.

Parental duties:

There is general consensus around parents providing the basic necessities, with increasing interest in children's rights within the home environment.

Providing physical security:

Providing physical security refers to a safety of a child's body, safety of a child's life, physical safety: shelter, clothes, nourishment, protect a child from dangers; physical care and care for a child's health.

Providing physical development:

Developing a child physically refers to providing conditions to a healthy growth of a child, provide a child with the means to develop physically, train the body of a child, to introduce to sport, develop habits of health, and physical games.

Providing intellectual security:

Intellectual security refers to the conditions, in which a child's mind can develop. If the child's dignity is safe, that is nobody encroaches upon a child physically or verbally, then he is able to learn, provide an atmosphere of peace and justice in family, where no one's dignity is encroached upon, provide "no-fear," "no-threat, "no-verbal abuse" environment, and spend bonding times and share wonderful moments with children.

Providing intellectual development:

Intellectual development means providing opportunity to a child to learn - to learn about laws of nature and moral laws, reading, writing, calculating etc, intellectual games, social skills and etiquette, moral and spiritual development, ethics and value systems, and norms and contributions to the child's belief and cultural customs.

Providing emotional security:

To provide security to a child is to help protect and shield the child's fragile psyche. It is to provide a safe loving environment, give a child a sense of being loved, being needed, welcomed, give a child a sense of being loved through, emotional support, encouragement, and caressing, hugging, touch, etc.

Providing emotional development:

Development refers to giving a child an opportunity to love other people, to care, to help. Developing in a child a ability to love through, showing empathy and compassion to younger and older, weaker and sicker, etc, and caring for others, helping grandparents, etc.

Other parental duties:

Financial support: Money provided as child support by custodial or non-custodial parent(s), or the state. Insurance coverage and payments for education

Parenting models, tools, philosophies and practices:

Conventional models of parenting:

"Rules of traffic" models:

It is an instructional approach to upbringing. Parents explain to their children how to behave, assuming that they taught the rules of behavior as they did the rules of traffic. What you try to teach a child doesn't necessarily mean it'll get through to them. For example, a teenager was told "a thousand times" that stealing was wrong yet the teen continued to do so. The problem of parenting, in this case, is not that they tried to teach him/her the right thing, but that they considered parenting as a single, narrow minded method of parenting, without fulfilling the range of parental duties.

"Fine gardening" model:

Parents believe that children have positive and negative qualities, the latter of which parents should "weed out" or "prune" into an appropriate shape. The problem in this parenting method is that parents fight with the faults of their child rather than appreciate their current achievements and/or capabilities; a method which may continue through their whole life without success.

"The models "rules of traffic" and "fine gardening" are especially dangerous because we, following our best motives, constantly quarrel with our children; destroy relationships, and all our parental work becomes a hopeless effort. Moreover, we don't understand why this has happened." S.Soloveychik.

"Reward and punishment" model:

"RaP" is a most popular model of parenting based on logic: for a good action - a reward/praise for a bad action - a punishment/scolding/reprimand. To teach a child by this logic is relatively easy and can even be effective, especially if it is done consistently. It is because it forms a sense of justice in a child's mind that it works. But, simultaneously, it imparts the child's universal image of the reward and punishment and when real life doesn't prove to be just it undermines the child's faith in justice, according to S.Soloveychik. He writes "It is dangerous for the future of children. It may happen that a man, grown up by this model, facing the first serious failure or first trouble, would lift his arms and ask, "Why me?"

Modern models of parenting:

Parenting typically utilizes tools of reward and punishment method, but most child development experts now agree that corporal punishment is not an effective behavior modification tool. In some jurisdictions corporal punishment (e.g., spanking or whipping) has been prohibited by law. Many parents have adopted non-physical approaches to child discipline, for example time-out. The other "civilized" forms of discipline behavioral control, structure, accountability, Parental supervision, etc.

Examples of modern parenting models:

"Nurturing":

This is a family model where children are expected to explore their surroundings with protection from their parents.

"Strict father model":

Places a strong value on discipline as a means to survive and thrive in a harsh world.

"Attachment parenting":

Seeks to create strong emotional bonds, avoiding physical punishment and accomplishing discipline through interactions recognizing a child's emotional needs all while focusing on holistic understanding of the child.

"Taking Children Seriously":

Sees both praise and punishment as manipulative and harmful to children and advocates other methods to reach agreement with them.

"Parenting For Everyone":

The philosophy of Parenting for Everyone considers parenting from the ethical point of view. It analyses parenting goals, conditions and means of childrearing. It offers to look at a child's internal world (emotions, intelligence and spirit) and derive the sources of parenting success from there. The concept of heart implies the child's sense of being loved and their ability to love others. The concept of intelligence implies the child's morals. And the concept of spirit implies the child's desire to do good actions and avoid bad behavior, avoid encroaching upon anybody's dignity. The core concept of the philosophy of Parenting for Everyone is the concept of dignity, the child's sense of worthiness and justice.

Christian parenting:

In the United States, disparate models explicitly termed "Christian parenting" are popular among some parents who claim to apply biblical principles to parenting. Information on Christian parenting is found in publications, Christian parenting websites, and in seminars devoted to helping parents apply Christian principles to parenting.

While some Christian parenting models are strict and authoritarian, others are "grace-based" and share methods advocated in attachment parenting and positive parenting theories. Particularly influential on opposite sides have been James Dobson and his book Dare to Discipline, and William Sears who has written several parenting books including The Complete Book of Christian Parenting & Child Care and The Discipline Book.

In a study of Christian parents done by Christian Parenting Today in 2000, 39% of the families surveyed have family devotions once a week or more, and 69% of parents consider Sunday school, youth and children's programs extremely important.

Parenting issues across the child's lifespan:

Planning and Pre-pregnancy:

This is family planning decisions about whether and when to become parents, planning, preparing, and gathering resources. Reproductive health and preconception care affect pregnancy, reproductive success and maternal and child health.

Pregnancy and prenatal parenting:

During pregnancy the unborn child is affected by many decisions his or her parents make, particularly choices linked to their lifestyle. The health and diet decisions of the mother can have either a positive or negative impact on the child during prenatal parenting.

Many people believe that parenting begins with birth, but the mother begins raising and nurturing a child well before birth. Scientific evidence indicates that from the fifth month on, the unborn baby is able to hear sound, be aware of motion, and possibly exhibit short-term memory. Several studies (e.g. Kissilevsky et al., 2003) show evidence that the unborn baby can become familiar with his or her parents' voices. Other research indicates that by the seventh month, external schedule cues influence the unborn baby's sleep habits. Based on this evidence, parenting actually begins well before birth.

Depending on how many children the mother carries also determines the amount of care needed during prenatal and post-natal periods.

James E. Rummel

Infants:

Being the parent of an infant is a major responsibility. Infants require dedicated care, including (but not limited to) feeding, bathing, changing diapers, and health care. Because of this, you would be wise to be committed to this child's well-being, since the rest of your life will have to be centered on it.

Toddlers:

Parenting a toddler requires time and hard work. Parenting responsibilities during the toddler years include (but are not limited to) feeding, bathing, potty training, ensuring safety, teaching, and attending to the well-being of the child. Parenting toddlers also requires emotionally sound parents and guardians. Toddlers are basically older infants and require the same if not more patience.

Preschoolers:

Parents are expected to make important decisions about preschool education and early childhood education. Parents have to love and care for their preschoolers doing all that they can to keep them safe. It is important not to keep things lying around that are dangerous to small children and items that say keep out of reach of children. Children at this age are very likely to put things in their mouths and eat and drink things that are dangerous to their health.

Elementary and Middle School Years:

Parenting issues related to parenting school age children include Education, Kindergarten, and Primary education. Parents must also gear them for the school years to come, which require emotional toughness.

Adolescents:

During adolescence children are beginning to form their identity and are testing and developing the interpersonal and occupational roles that they will assume as adults. Although adolescents look to peers and adults outside of the family for guidance and models for how to behave, parents remain influential in their development. Parents should make efforts to be aware of their adolescent's activities, provide guidance, direction, and consultation. Adolescence can be a time of high risk for children, where newfound freedoms can result in decisions that drastically open up or close off life opportunities. Parental issues at this stage of parenting include dealing with "rebellious" teenagers, who didn't know freedom while they were smaller.

Young Adults:

When grown-up children become adults their personalities show the result of successful or unsuccessful parenting. Especially it is noticeable when young adults make their independent life decisions about their education, work and choosing mates for friendship or marriage.

Adults and Older Adults:

Parenting doesn't stop when children grow up and age. Parents always remain to be parents for old children. Their relationship continues developing if both parties want to keep it or improve. The parenting issues may include the relationship with grandchildren and children-in-law.

Chapter 17 — Emotions/Feelings:

Some people have a problem knowing what they are feeling or what emotions they have. Or you may be able to identify the feelings and emotions but are unable to express them. When feelings and emotions begin to come up in the course of facing phobias or dealing with panic, there is often a tendency to withhold them, which only aggravates your stress and anxiety. The purposes of this chapter is to help you increase your awareness of feelings and to give you some tools and strategies for identifying and expressing them more readily.

Facts about Feelings and Emotions:

Feelings and emotions, unlike thoughts, involve a total body reaction. They are mediated both by a part of your brain called the limbic system and the involuntary, autonomic nervous system in your body. When you're emotionally excited, you feel it all over and experience bodily reactions such as increased heart rate, respiration, perspiration, and even shaking or trembling (note the similarity to panic, which is another type of intense emotional state).

Feelings do not come out of the blue but are influenced by your thoughts and perceptions. They arise from the way you perceive or interpret outer events and/or the way you react to your own inner thought processes or self-talk, imagery, or memories. If you can't identify a stimulus for a particular emotional reaction (for example, a spontaneous panic attack), that stimulus may be unconscious. Feelings are also affected by stress. When you're under stress, your body is already in a state of physiological arousal similar to that which accompanies an emotion. Since you're already primed to have emotional reactions, it may not take much to set you off. The particular type of emotion you happen to experience will depend on your view of external events and what you tell yourself about them.

Feelings can be divided into two groups – simple and complex. There is much controversy and disagreement about how to do this – and even whether it can be done – but for our purposes here, a distinction will be made between basic emotions such as anger, grief, sadness, fear, love, excitement, or joy, and more complex feelings such as eagerness, relief, disappointment, or impatience. Complex feelings may involve a combination of more basic emotions and are also shaped by thoughts and imagery. Many of the feelings on the Feeling List are complex. Complex feelings can last a long time and are more tied to thought processes, while basic emotions tend to be short-lived, more reactive, and more tied to involuntary physical reactions mediated by the autonomic nervous system. Fear or panic is a basic emotion while free-floating anxiety (anxiety without an object) is an example of a more complex feeing.

Feelings are what give you energy. If you're in touch with your feelings and can express them, you'll feel more energetic. If you're out of touch with your feelings or unable to give them expression, you may feel lethargic, numb, tired, or depressed. Blocked or withheld feelings can lead to anxiety.

Feelings often come in mixtures rather than in pure form. Sometimes you may experience a simple, basic emotion such as fear, sadness, or rage. More often, though, you'll find that you feel two or more emotions at the same time. For example, it's common to feel anger and fear at the same time when you're threatened. Or you may feel anger, guilt, and love all at the same time in response to arguing with your partner, parent, or close friend. The common expression sorting out feelings reflects the fact that you can feel several things at once.

Feelings are often contagious. If you're close to someone who is crying, you may start to feel sad or even cry yourself. Or you may pick up on another's excitement or enthusiasm. Phobic and anxiety-prone individuals are often particularly susceptible to taking on the feelings of people around them. The more you learn to be in touch with and comfortable with your own feelings, the less prone you'll be to catch those of others.

Feelings are not right or wrong. As reactions, feelings simply exist. Fear, joy, guilt, or anger are not in and of themselves valid or invalid

– you just happen to have these feelings and usually will feel better if you can express them. The perceptions or judgments you made which led to your feelings, however, may be right or wrong, valid or invalid. Be careful not to make yourself or anyone else wrong for simply having a feeling, whatever that feeling may be.

Feelings are often subject to suppression. Sometimes you may actively control or hold in your feelings. For example, you're still upset from an argument with your spouse and then you have to talk to a colleague at work. You deliberately and consciously hold back your feelings, because you know that it would be inappropriate for them to carry over into your work situation. On other occasions, you may start to experience feelings that are unpleasant and decide that you don't want to deal with them. Instead of deliberately suppressing them, you just get busy and put your mind on something else – in existence you ignore them. This avoidance or evasion of feelings is a sublet form of suppression (which some people speak of as repression). Over time, the practice of continually suppressing your feelings can lead to increased difficulty in expressing or even identifying them. When the process of suppression begins in childhood, you tend to grow up being out of touch with your feelings and going through life experiencing a certain numbness or emptiness.

Identifying Your Feelings:

Identify your feelings by recognizing the symptoms of suppressed feelings, tune in to your body, and discriminate the exact feeling. Suppressed feelings frequently make themselves known through several types of bodily and psychological symptoms such as anxiety, depression, psychosomatic symptoms, and muscle tension.

Anxiety:

Anxiety arises from many sources. Sometimes it's simply fear in the face of uncertainty. Sometimes it's the result of anticipating a negative outcome (what-if thinking). If anxiety doesn't seem to relate to any specific situation – if it's only a vague, underlined uneasiness – this may be because it arises from strong but unexpressed feelings. Every feeling carries a charge of energy. When we hold that energy in and do not give it expression, it may create a state of tension or vague anxiety. The next time you hold in your anger toward someone, notice whether you feel anxious afterward. Holding in enthusiasm or excitement about something can also produce anxiety.

Depression:

In his well-known book, The Road Less Traveled, M. Scott Peck defines depression as stuck feelings. Often we feel depressed when we're holding in unexpressed grief or sadness over some loss. Letting out tears and crying often helps us to feel better – we effectively mourn the loss. Depression can also result from holding in anger. Gestalt psychologists were the first to point out that depression can mask anger turned in against the self. If you find yourself feeling depressed without any obvious recent loss, it may help to ask yourself what you're angry about. This is an especially good question if you find that you're attacking and criticizing yourself. Extreme depression can lead to suicide.

Anger:

Anger is an emotional state that varies from mild irritation to intense fury or rage. You might know when you are angry when you look in the mirror, your shoulders or jaws are tight, your heart is beating faster, you are feeling nervous, you are yelling, or you start to sweat. You might control your anger by asking yourself will the object of my anger matter ten years from now, did that person do this to me on purpose, count to ten before saying anything, visualize a relaxing experience, remind yourself that getting angry is not going to fix anything if no one is listening, try to use humor, go to another room away from what is angering you, yell into a pillow, call a friend that will listen and help you understand why you are so angry, never take your anger out on another person that had nothing to do with you being angry in the first place, and/or go for a walk.

Some causes of anger are frustration, hurt, annoyance, disappointment, harassment, and threats. The body reacts to anger by the heart pumping faster, blood pressure rising, and/or muscles tense. Anger can help us reach our goals; however, it must be managed. It is a normal emotion. It can be managed by recognizing it, identifying the cause, and decide what to do about it. Uncontrolled anger can lead to crime, abuse, and violent behavior, such as throwing things, and self mutilation or suicide.

Recognize the anger by paying attention to the signs of hidden anger such as tense muscles, upset stomach, tendency to use bad sarcasm, rigid posture, sweating, and/or rapid pulse. In identifying the cause it may not be what it seems at first. You must decide which options will resolve the problem or situation. Take positive steps to implement those options. Keep your cool when you communicated your anger. Try to calm down once you have released your anger, understand motives or reasons for your anger, assert yourself, and seek help if you need to. Don't get personal, avoid the issue, accuse, or sulk. You need to find a solution to what is causing you to be angry in the first place.

Other ways to control anger are humor, physical activity, rest, relaxation, or maybe writing a feelings journal. If you count to ten, take a long breathe, say number one to yourself, relax your entire body as you breath out, and repeat these things until you calm down. You need to release the anger and stress of the situation.

Psychosomatic Symptoms:

Common psychosomatic symptoms such as headaches, ulcers, high blood pressure, and asthma are often the end result of chronically withheld feelings. While psychosomatic symptoms can arise from any type of chronic stress, the holding in of feelings over many years is a form of stress that is especially likely to take its toll on your body. Learning to identify and express strong feelings can lead to a reduction or even a remission of many types of psychosomatic symptoms. Find a way to release these feelings and relax. Trauma is a reaction to these withheld feelings and psychological abuse.

Muscle Tension:

Stiff, tight muscles are an especially common symptom of chronically withheld feelings. We tend to tighten certain groups of muscles when we suppress and hold in what we feel. Different feelings are held in by tightening different muscle groups. Anger or frustration is often suppressed by tightening the back of your neck and shoulders.

(These are the areas, incidentally, where tension is most commonly experienced in our society). Grief and sadness can be held in by tightening muscles in the chest and around the eyes. Fear can be held in through tightening up in the stomach-diaphragm area. Withheld sexual feelings may be indicated by a tightening up of muscle groups in the pelvic region.

These correlations between areas of the body and suppression of specific feelings should not be viewed as absolute. Anger, for example, can be held in by tightening many different muscle groups from the eyes to the pelvis. The point is that tight muscles and physical tension in any region may be a sign of chronically bottled-up feelings. This relationship between suppressed feelings and muscular tension has been explored in great depth by the school of therapy known as Bioenergetics. The books of Dr. Alexander Lowen provide a good introduction to this approach.

Tuning into your Body:

Staying in your head preoccupied with daily worries and concerns tend to keep you out of touch with your feelings. To switch gears and gain access to your feelings, it's necessary to shift your focus from your head to your body. Feelings tend to be held in the body. Our use of language reflects this in expressions such as heart-broken, pain in the neck, and gut-level feeling. By making time to tune into your body you can learn to get in touch with and identify your feelings. Many people have found physical relaxation, questioning yourself about your feelings, tuning into your body, and wait and listen to what your feelings say.

Physically Relax:

It's difficult to know what you're feeling if your body is tense and your min is racing. Spend 5-10 minutes doing progressive muscle relaxation, meditation, or some other relaxation technique to slow you down.

Question yourself about your feelings:

Ask yourself, what am I feeling right now? Alternately, ask yourself, what is my main problem or concern right now?

Tuning into your body:

Tune in to that place in your body where you feel emotional sensations such as anger, fear, or sadness. Often this will be in the area of your heart or your gut (stomach/diaphragm), although it may be other areas higher or lower in the body. This is your inner place of feelings.

Wait and Listen:

Wait and listen to whatever you can sense or pick up on in your place of feelings. Don't try to analyze or judge what's there. Be an observer and allow yourself to sense any feelings or moods that are waiting to surface. Simply wait until something emerges.

Expressing Feelings:

Once you're able to identify what you're feeling, it's very important to express it. Expressing feelings, here, is defined as letting them out by sharing them with someone else, writing them out, or physically discharging them (such as by hitting a plastic bat against your bed or crying into a pillow). Expressing your feelings does not mean dumping or directing them toward someone you perceive to be responsible for how you feel. The skill of letting someone know how you feel about them (or better, their behavior).

Feelings can be compared to charges of energy that need physical release or discharge from the body. When unexpressed, they tend to be stored in your body in the form of tension, anxiety, or other symptoms previously described. Your physical health as well as your sense of well-being depends on your willingness to acknowledge and express feelings at or close to the time they occur. Here are some useful ways of expressing your feelings.

Talk it out:

Probably the best way to express feelings is to share them with a supportive friend, mate, or counselor. Sharing your feelings means not just talking about your feelings by actually letting them out. It's important that you have a high level of trust toward the person you share with in order to open up and fully disclose your true feelings. And it's important that they listen carefully – in other words, they do not offer advice, opinions, or suggestions while you're sharing. Your ability to share will in part be determined by your partner's willingness to do nothing more than just listen. (This type of listening may still be active, where the listener occasionally summarizes what you've said in order to confirm that it's been correctly understood).

Write it out:

If your feelings are running high and there's no one immediately available to talk to, take a pen and paper and write out what you feel. You may wish to keep a feeling journal in which you enter your strong feelings from time t o time. Weeks or months later it will be very instructive to go back and read through the journal to get an idea of broad patterns or themes running through your life. Whether you keep a journal or not, the act of writing out your feelings will often suffice as an outlet until you have the opportunity to talk them out.

Discharging Sadness:

You might want to ask yourself the following questions, do you ever cry?, under what circumstances do you cry?, do you cry because someone hurt you, because you feel lonely, or because you're scared?, do you cry for no apparent reason?, or do you only cry alone or do you permit other people to see you crying?

Sometimes you may have a feeling of being on the verge of tears. You feel like you would like to cry but are having difficulty getting it out. At this point you may find that a particular artistic prodding will help. Evocative pieces of music that have personal significance can often help to elicit tears. Watching an emotional movie or reading poetry or literature or even certain television commercials may also bring an initially vague sense of sadness to the surface.

Self Esteem Tips:

For your self esteem, identify your fears. Challenges can be scary, but your fears are usually much worse than reality. Forget your failures and learn from them and move on. Avoid making the same mistakes again, you're wiser and stronger now; don't be trapped in your past. Know what you want and don't be afraid to ask for it. Maybe you don't know what it is you want, take some time and figure it out, talk to others, journal, explore your options. Reward yourself when you succeed. Maybe it's you walked on treadmill or you cleaned your room. Be proud of your accomplishments each day. Talk, ask questions, and talk more. Don't assume, just because you think so it doesn't mean it is. Don't be defeated, try something else. No one is good at everything. Focus on your strengths and learn from your mistakes, try again, or try a different way.

Beliefs that will not cause Problems:

Everyone doesn't have to love me and it is okay to make mistakes. Other people are ok and I am ok. I don't have to control things and I am responsible for my day. I can handle it when things go wrong and it is important to always try. Say I am capable and can take care of myself. I can change and other people are capable. Also you want to try to be flexible. Have an opinion and make good decisions. Live life right and you stand a better chance of living longer. Be truthful with yourself and others so that you might have a clear conscience. It's okay to make mistakes, but it is important to recover. Try to make good friends that will support you when you get into trouble or need help.

Chapter 18 – Concluding Remarks:

From the previous chapters you can see what the basic of life are and how they can mold or shape your life and give you points of reference for your decisions and choice whether it be politics, science, or whatever.

www.ingramcontent.com/pod-product-compliance
Lightning Source LLC
Chambersburg PA
CBHW020251290526
45784CB00003B/1193